What people are saying about MYSTERIOUS CALIFORNIA:

"A terrric book... really fascinating!" — *Paul Wallach, KIEV RADIO*

"Oddments off the well-worn tourist path." — *LOS ANGELES TIMES BOOK REVIEW*

"Who could resist a book about ghosts and haunted houses, especially if it includes directions on how and where to find them? Mike Marinacci's **MYSTERIOUS CALIFORNIA: Strange Places and Eerie Phenomena in the Golden State** is the first travel guide to more than 100 California locations that emphasizes anomalies." — *THE FRESNO BEE*

"A very comprehensive job of guiding us to...all of the rather strange and mysterious places that exist, and there are far more than I knew!" — *Dick Whittington, KIEV RADIO*

"Anyone unfamiliar with the state's rich heritage of mystery, which goes way beyond Bigfoot and Mount Shasta, will be happy to add this particular book to his library." — *FATE MAGAZINE*

"You simply cannot put it down...a wonderful piece of work." — *Ken Kramer, KSDO RADIO*

"A valuable service for...connoisseurs of the unusual." — *STRANGE MAGAZINE*

"A great haunting of a book." — *THE BOOK READER*

MYSTERIOUS CALIFORNIA

Strange Places and
Eerie Phenomena
in the Golden State

by Mike Marinacci

PANPIPES PRESS
Los Angeles, California

First Printing, September 1988
Second Printing, July 1989

ISBN 0-929046-02-1
Library of Congress Card No.: 88-090694

Cover and Chapter Headings by Rudy Marinacci
Layout by Mike Marinacci
Typesetting by ByteType, Santa Monica, Calif.
Printed in the United States of America

Photo Credits All photos © 1988 by Mike Marinacci, except **28**: Patterson &
Gimlin, © Rene Dahinden; **47**: Winchester Mystery House, San Jose, Calif.; **50**:
University of California at Santa Cruz, Library Special Collections; **68**: James
Ginney (National Park Service); **115 (upper)**: Robert F. Heizer (UCLA Rock Art
Archives).
Drawing of the "Billiwack Monster" (P. 85) by Bob Beebe.

Table of Contents

Introduction

I am aware of the fact that no Chamber of Commerce in any of the very progressive cities of California would think of writing a book about the local allurements of each community by giving any emphasis to the weird sights, strange sounds or peculiar mysteries within its own borders...But to the lover of mystery, the student of the sciences, the research worker, the thinker, and those intellectually inclined, the mysteries of California are not only appealing but never completely solved and never forgotten.

Harve Spencer Lewis,
Lemuria, the Lost
Continent of the
Pacific (1931)

When Mr. Lewis, writing as Wishar Cerve, penned those words a half-century ago, California was already America's strangest state.

Spanish explorers were the first outsiders to note the land's otherworldly qualities. Mistaking the mountainous land mass north of Mexico for an island, the 16th-century *conquistadores* named it California, after a fictional island utopia ruled by a black queen named Califa.

There were no black queens on the would-be island that was early California. Instead, there were many Indian tribes who told tales that were just as fantastic, legends that were ancient when the first white men walked onto the Golden State's shores.

The natives told tales of the strange race of beings that lived inside snow-capped, solitary Mount Shasta in the northeast. Tribes in the dark forests of northwest California whispered of huge, half-human beasts that shambled through the wilderness. Others spoke of inland lakes haunted by serpentine creatures that sometimes stuck their long necks out of the murky waters and terrified lake-dwelling humans. These legends almost disappeared with the peoples who told them, until recent years, when latter-day Californians unaware of native traditions began to tell strangely similar stories about the same places.

The old legends may have almost faded away, but California's newcomers created their own lore and mysteries. The Spanish missions, built to Christianize and "civilize" the Indians, were also scenes of bloodshed, tragedy and intrigue. The padres and their flocks abandoned all the old adobe chapels and dormitories, but the tales of ghostly monks, headless horsemen, curses and buried treasure still linger, eerie reminders of the state's romantic Iberian past.

Mexico, a young nation with ancient roots, held California next as part of Aztlan Province. With the Mexican settlers came their patron bogey-woman, *La Llorona*, who was sometimes spotted dipping her bloodstained arms in creek waters around what is now Orange County. But Mexico soon lost the province to American Manifest Destiny, and the land became fertile ground for a new mythology to take root.

The Gold Rush, with all its attendant greed-poisoned fantasies, boom-town lunacy and violence, made the word "Californian" almost synonymous with crazed dream-chasing (a stereotype still popular in most of America). Prospectors searching for the elusive Mother Lode told tales of stranger treasures found in the hills and canyons: rocks covered with the writings of vanished races, ancient ships run aground on the low desert, mountain tunnels filled with bizarre treasures and giant human skeletons.

Those who stayed in settled regions contributed to California's mysteries as well. Frontier violence and frontier justice held sway in the 19th-century big cities as well as in the mining camps, and modern residents swear that certain old hotels, houses and highways are haunted by murdered miners and lynched criminals, their ghosts still playing the tragic, bloody roles that they had in life.

As American civilization settled over the Golden State near the end of the 19th century, a new kind of dreamer began to migrate West. These were not pioneers out to tame the land for mining and farming, but visionaries seeking freedom and enlightenment. Victimized by uptight, Victorian mainstream America, they saw California as a new, wide-open world. If they wanted to eat only vegetables, walk around nude, meditate or communicate with Enlightened Masters or Space Brothers, there was plenty of beautiful open land for doing so. And in a state already filled with mavericks and individualists, they would fit right in.

Hundreds of new religions, sects, cults and ashrams sprung up in California, either imported or grown out of the fertile environment of social eccentricity and tolerance. The Theosophists, New Agers almost a century ahead of their time, made San Diego's Point Loma their headquarters for many years. The Rosicrucians, purveyors of Egyptian, Classical and Hermetic secret wisdom, are still centered in a parklike San Jose compound. Countless free-love, communalistic and renegade Christian sects have also lived and died here, from the mid-1850s all the way up to the approaching Millennium.

The state's location on the Pacific Rim made it a natural recipient of Eastern wisdom as well. Japanese Zen Masters and East Indian gurus made California their traditional first stop in North America. Some, like Krishnamurti, stayed on for good.

Even pragmatic, rationalistic scientists have always been lured to the enigmatic Golden State. Geologists have been intrigued with and puzzled by such earth mysteries as Death Valley's "moving rocks," San Joaquin Valley's peculiar "hog wallow" mounds, and the erratic boulders at Point Loma. Seismologists studying the earthquake-ridden state have noted such odd phenomena as Hollister's "earthquake lights." And archeologists have debated heatedly, even acrimoniously, over the lonely spot in the Mojave Desert that may be the remnant of a 200,000 year-old human tool works.

And the average non-scientist, non-mystic Californian is not immune to the state's strangeness. Though development has covered much of the land, suburbs, shopping malls and interstate freeways seem to just bring residents ever closer to the mysteries. Urbanization didn't stop a hairy, giant ape-thing from terrifying apartment dwellers in Buena Park. Or halt the ghostly "Woman in Black"'s forays through downtown Monterey's Stevenson House. Or obliterate the curious, ancient networks of walls that lie just beyond East Bay suburbia in the Oakland Hills.

This book is a guide to over 100 sites in California where strange, bizarre, inexplicable and eerie phenomena have occurred. Some sites are notorious. A few are world-renowned. Others are little known to the general public. The book covers everything from famous and not-so-famous haunted houses, to places of legend, to the reputed lairs of monsters and strange beasts, to scientific anomalies, to weird cult centers. All of the places listed and described here are accessible to the public, or at least can be seen from a close distance; many are relatively unknown, not yet restricted by public park systems or exploited by private interests.

A Note on Site Selection and Organization

The places in *Mysterious California* were selected from several hundred possible candidates, the result of over a year of extensive research and fieldwork.

For a number of reasons, many phenomena and places have been excluded. UFO sightings are mostly absent here, since they tend to be erratic and transitional and aren't consistently reported at specific places, as ghosts or mystery animals are. Privately owned houses or lands are not in this book either, save for those that operate as businesses. A few sites were excluded because of space considerations. And quite a few places don't appear here simply because the author didn't know about them, despite his exhaustive research.

For the purposes of this book, California has been divided into three sections: **Northern**, starting at the Oregon border and extending to the county lines around the 37th Parallel; **Central**, between the 37th Parallel and Los Angeles and San Bernardino counties' northern lines; and **Southern**, the region between the latter boundaries and the Mexican border.

Each section is divided by counties, the most exact and logical subclasses. Counties in each region are arranged alphabetically. Individual listings are by city, town, park or geographical features, with exact locations detailed in the listings. Hard-to-find sites have more explicit directions given at the end of each entry.

Tips for Travelers

Though this book strives to be as accurate and up-to-date and possible, errors may have crept in here and there. Also, by the time you read this, some sites might be closed to the public or otherwise made inaccessible. When in doubt about a site, inquire locally.

Local inquiry is also recommended when venturing into remote desert or mountain regions. Road conditions and weather have a way of changing rapidly and disastrously, particularly in the Mojave Desert. Hunters of mystery who intend to stray from major paved roads should make careful preparations beforehand. Several of the sites listed here are churches and graveyards. Please show these places due respect. Though they might suffer disturbances from the Other World, they're still deserving of consideration from those in this one. Finally, *please* take care when visiting California's ancient sites. Most of the petroglyphs, pictographs, desert figures and stone ruins left by the state's native peoples were abused enough over the centuries by the elements, and have been further defaced by inconsiderate souvenir hunters, vandals and off-road vehicles.

Some Final Words and Acknowledgments

During his travels around the state compiling material for this book, the author was often asked if he "believed" any of the stories and legends about ghosts, monsters, etc.. He usually answered by saying that he didn't "believe" or "disbelieve" any of them. There are a lot of places, he said, such as San Diego's Whaley House, where something genuinely inexplicable is going on. And there are plenty of stories that seem pretty unlikely, like the one about Los Angeles' "underground city." Most of the phenomena and theories that he came across seemed to be "maybes," mysteries that might never be solved to anyone's satisfaction.

The important thing is that the places are part of a collective mythology peculiar to California, a mythology created by the state's many peoples that reflects their hopes and fears, and their dreams and nightmares. Whether the legends are of primeval monsters or of extraterrestrials, they take on a life of their own in the collective Californian mind. As someone once remarked about UFOs, even if they don't really exist, the tremendous effect their story has had on the modern world still makes them important.

Now, some acknowledgements are due. This guide to California's places of myth and wonder could not have been put together without the assistance of the following people:

Firstly, these five men inspired the author with their own studies of the strange, the inexplicable and the anomalous, and they should be thanked for their tremendous influence on him and others who probe the fringes of reality: Jim Brandon, Loren Coleman, the late Charles Fort, John Keel and Robert Anton Wilson.

Next comes the largest group, the people who helped the author track down books, articles and photographs of Golden State anomalies, or just provided informational, materiel and/or psychic assistance: Brikti Abraha, Monica Bontty, Janet Bord, Mark Chorvinsky (STRANGE Magazine), Barbara Clarke, David Costa, June Crawley (UCSC Special Collections Library), Rene Dahinden, Al Fry, Shirley Harding (Death Valley National Monument), Mark Hendrix, Dr. Barclay Kamb (Cal-Tech), Ken Kelly, Raymond Manners (International Fortean Organization), Helen Michaelis (UCLA Rock Art Archives), Ronald Miller, Mary Newton, Dean Oisboid, John and Karen Reynolds, Judith Richlin-Klonsky, Dr. Nina Schneider (UCLA), Diane Schocker (Willow Creek Tourist Information Center), Richard Senate, Lenny Shaw, Michael Villano, Jane Way, Charlene Weber, Jane Wildhorn, Margaret Zamorano, and the staffs of the California State University at Fullerton's Library Special Collections; the East California Museum; and the UCLA Research Library's Interlibrary Loan, Reference and Special Collections departments.

Finally, the author must give the greatest thanks of all to his parents, Rudy and Barbara Marinacci. Themselves authors of two books of California history and travel, this work would have been impossible without their considerable assistance in all areas. This book is dedicated to them.

A final note: The author welcomes all criticisms, suggestions, corrections and contributions that readers might want to send, and will *try* to personally answer all of them. Please address all correspondence to:

Michael Marinacci
c/o Panpipes Press
P.O. Box 25226
Los Angeles, CA 90025-0226

I. Northern California

ALAMEDA COUNTY

Berkeley: *The University of California* UC Berkeley, the hub of the state university system, boasts a population of 30,000 students, and at least two ghosts.

The more famous one lives in Room 19 of the Faculty Club. Guests there have reported strange encounters with a "gentlemanly" old man who sits in a chair and stares at them silently. He's thought to be the spirit of a professor who lived in the room from 1935 to 1971; apparently, his tenure extends beyond the grave. Room occupants also say that something looking like "two heads with a body" floats around the room.

Another haunt is at Sather bell tower, where a student once jumped to his death. A "spirit photograph" taken of the lawn below the tower revealed a fuzzy, disembodied hand reaching out of the ground. A noted psychic investigator examined the photograph later and, though normally skeptical of such camerawork, believed there was something about the "phantom limb" picture that was eerily convincing.

ALPINE COUNTY

Markleeville The highways and mountain passes around this little East

Sierran village have long been haunted by a Civil War soldier in full battle dress. Those who have seen the ghostly trooper say he wears a blue Union uniform, and is unarmed. When confronted by the living, he stares at them, walks away slowly...and disappears before their eyes.

Nobody knows who the soldier is, or why he patrols the lonely region. He just marches on, oblivious to death and the passage of a century.

AMADOR COUNTY

Sutter Creek: *The Sutter Creek Inn (75 Main St.)* Jane Way, owner and proprietor of this New England-style bed-and-breakfast inn, is surely one of the warmest and friendliest innkeepers one would want to meet in California's Gold Country. Perhaps that's why a ghostly exhibitionist sought her out for help.

Jane recalls that she was sitting in the front office one day when a strange man peeked around the door. Moments later, he dropped his pants, displayed his considerable endowments and vanished.

Though shocked, Jane, a practicing spiritualist, realized that the phantom flasher was a troubled, traumatized soul seeking to rid himself of the hangups and neuroses that held him to the spirit world. She got the impression that the man was a local character who had finally been castrated because of his behavior (somehow, he had gotten his goodies

A ghostly exhibitionist once appeared at the Sutter Creek Inn.

back in the next world). She therefore held a seance to "clear and cleanse" him of his burdens, so that he could move on to the Other Side. He hasn't been seen since.

Such encounters were nothing new to Ms. Way, who had been having strange experiences in the house since she bought it in 1966. The house was the former home of State Senator Edward Voorhies, and she says that just after she moved in, his benevolent spirit appeared and told her, "I will protect your inn."

There's the specter of an old woman, too, though she's less amiable. One night, an invisible force picked up Jane's cat and threw it violently against the wall. The cat survived the attack, but Jane was frightened and puzzled by the attack. A medium who visited the house identified the force as the ghost of a cat-hating elderly woman. Like the exhibitionist, she had brought her psychological problems to the spirit world.

Confident in her own growing skills as a medium, and mindful of the spiritualist belief many old houses have resident entities, Jane continues to run the Sutter Creek Inn unafraid of the unpaying, unseen permanent guests that reside there.

BUTTE COUNTY

Chico Something up there doesn't like this Sacramento Valley town. Years ago, for some unimaginable reason, Chico was pelted by rocks, fish and huge meteorites from on high.

The town's most celebrated round of troubles with mysterious falling objects happened in 1921. Late in that year, huge, unexplained showers of rocks began to rain on two warehouses standing at what is now the corner of 6th and Orange.

In January 1922, Chico Marshal J.A. Peck received several official complaints about the strange pellets. Peck and his deputies spent two months investigating the odd phenomenon, but were baffled. On March 14, 1922, he told the *San Francisco Examiner* that he had seen and heard the stones fall, and decided that some local prankster "with a machine" was responsible. Police kept a sharp eye on one suspect, but when he was out of town, the rocks still kept falling.

By this time, crowds had begun to gather outside the warehouses to watch the peculiar hail. Witnesses noted that the rocks seemed to appear in midair and fall straight down, and that they were "warm" to the touch. A big deluge on March 17 injured a bystander.

One observer was a local scientist who found some strange facts about the rocks. Prof. C.K. Studley of Chico State College recovered some of the stones, and after analyzing them, said that they were not of meteoric origin. Two of them even showed signs of cementation. Professor Studley also believed that the rocks were too heavy to have been thrown by any ordinary means, since one of his specimens weighed a full pound. Fist-sized stones weren't the first objects to rain on Chico. The *Chico Record* of Sept. 2, 1878, reported that on August 20 of that year, a huge number of small fishes fell from a clear sky onto the town streets. They spread over several acres of the town and completely covered one store's roof. Seven years later, an iron meteorite weighing several tons plummeted to earth just east of town.

Oroville: *Cherokee Road (N of town)* On the afternoon of July 12, 1969, Charles Jackson and his son Kevin got the shock of their lives here. They were burning rabbit entrails in their backyard, when a huge, apelike creature loped out of the woods and stopped to stare at them.

The beast was seven to eight feet tall, had large breasts and was covered with three-inch-long grey hair except on its hands and face. The Jacksons, only 15 feet away at the time, said that after it spotted them, it walked up to the outhouse, looked around and suddenly ran back into the woods.

Another Cherokee Road resident had a run-in with the "apeman" around the same time as the Jackson incident. For weeks, Homer Stickley's farm had been haunted by something that screamed in the woods at night and stole apples from his trees. Then, one moonlit night, Stickley saw the culprit: a tall, hirsute two-legged creature who walked through a nearby meadow, pausing to stand by a stump.

By September, at least a dozen people had reported giant ape-things running around Oroville, but the Cherokee Road sightings remained the most documented and credible of the lot. Six years later, people were still seeing the beasts and finding their huge footprints in the area, but the creatures remained at large. By then, Oroville had established itself as another home of North America's most famous land monster, Bigfoot. (More on this oft-seen, never-captured creature in a few pages, under **HUMBOLDT COUNTY: Bluff Creek.**)

CALAVERAS COUNTY

Mokelumne Hill: *The Leger Hotel* Ronald Miller, historian, writer and proprietor of this Victorian hotel just off Highway 49, says the resident

Room 7, George's home at the Leger Hotel.

ghost is not a mysterious, terrifying apparition. Instead, the spirit is like an eccentric permanent guest. He's so much a part of hotel life that his name is mentioned whenever something goes wrong. If dishes fall and break, or if receipts disappear, or if there are just strange sounds late at night, it's George's fault.

"George" is George Leger, the hotel's 19th-century founder, who lived and died in Room 7, a small single upstairs. Obituaries of the period described him as a prominent, wealthy French immigrant, and say that he died after "a brief illness." Historians have their doubts though, and hint darkly about conspiracy, hired guns and murder.

Delving deeply into the hotel's history, Ronald Miller has found a history of odd "disturbances" there dating back to World War I. In his own tenure, several people, including his son, have seen a middle-aged, mustachioed man silently walking the halls. They always identify him afterwards as "the man in the picture in the office" (a period portrait of George Leger hangs there). Once, Ronald's son was playing noisily in the hall outside Room 7, when "the man" suddenly appeared, scolded the boy in a heavy Gallic accent, then vanished.

Guests that stay in or near Room 7 have often complained about unearthly footsteps and feminine giggling echoing through the deserted hallway after midnight. George was rumored to be a womanizer in his previous life; death seems not to have relieved him of his lusts. Knowing this, Ronald has hung some Victorian-era pin-ups on Room 7's wall for the randy spirit's enjoyment.

Ronald, his family and his employees have a special regard for the hotel's ghostly founder and namesake. George's presence is accepted as natural, if sometimes a little unnerving, and he's treated with respect and even affection.

Late one night, as he was making his last rounds of the hotel, Ronald was alone in a hallway when he saw two shadows on a wall—one of them his (he was wearing a cowboy hat at the time), and the other one of a bareheaded man. Instead of freezing in fear, he looked straight at the shadow and said quietly, "Goodnight, George," as he might to an old friend. The shadow vanished.

CONTRA COSTA COUNTY

Black Diamond Mines Regional Preserve Rose Hill Cemetery, a small burial ground above the 19th-century ghost towns of Nortonville and Somersville, bears silent testimony to the hardships and tragedy of life in this coal-mining region, formerly populated by hundreds of Welsh immigrants. Tombstones mark the resting places of men killed by mine disasters and black lung, of women who died in childbirth and of infants and small children felled by typhus and smallpox. Some of the headstones are lettered in Welsh, with flowery Celtic epitaphs to the departed.

But the sleep of the dead has been disturbed here. In recent years, vandals have opened graves and have toppled and smashed or stolen headstones. Most of the beautiful tombstones are either missing or broken.

This wanton desecration and destruction, some local psychics say, is what causes the eerie phenomena in and around Rose Hill Cemetery. Ghostly laughter, cries and the tolling of bells are sometimes heard coming from the graveyard. On still days, a windlike sound occasionally whispers through the cypress trees on the hill. Some people have seen a glowing cross hover slowly and silently above the night-darkened cemetery. And in one incident, a photographer in the graveyard was knocked down and menaced by an invisible force.

Rose Hill's best-known phantom is the "White Witch." Also known as "the Glowing Lady," or "the Gliding Woman," she's a luminous, white specter who glides above the field of headstones. One night she terrified a couple who had driven up to the cemetery for a tryst, when she floated right over to their parked car. Considering what's been done to the cemetery, one can hardly blame her for chasing off the living.

It seems that the Rose Hill phantoms are a persistent, unforgiving lot. Though each of the 119 known grave sites has been exorcised, the disturbances continue to this day.

Perhaps the living can yet make amends to the dead here. The Regional Parks service is currently trying to track down missing stones, repair extant ones, and generally help restore Rose Hill Cemetery to its pre-vandalism state. These good works may achieve what exorcism couldn't—bringing peace to the cemetery again.

Directions: From Concord, take Highway 4 east to the Loveridge Road exit, turn south, and then turn left at Buchanan. Turn right on Somersville, and drive to its end at the Preserve's parking lot. The trail to Rose Hill Cemetery starts there, and is about half a mile long.

Mount Diablo Early Spanish settlers aptly named this dark hump of land The Mountain of the Devil. There was something profoundly strange about the ominous peak, rearing up high above a wide plain. It seemed as if it might be home to things otherworldly and evil.

Diablo's original inhabitants also held the mountain in awe. The

Bolgones Indians claimed that the *Puy*—a devil—lived inside it, and that their shamans worked for him and his spirits.

When the two groups clashed, the mountain's spirit surfaced, and sided with the Indians. In 1806, Spanish General Mariano Vallejo was fighting the Bolgones in a hollow on Diablo's west side. Years later, he told the California legislature that in the midst of battle, a figure suddenly appeared alongside the Indians, clothed in bizarre plumage and making "divers movements." The Indians successfully fought off the Spaniards that day, and for months afterwards, the being appeared on the mountain slopes at the same time of day. The Indians were ultimately defeated in a later battle, and the apparition was seen no more.

But other odd phantoms took his place. In the fall of 1869, a hairy "wild man" was spotted running along the slopes of Crow Canyon, a few miles south of Diablo. Locals tried to catch him, but all they could find were his 13-inch footprints.

Diablo is also home to a large, black panther that sometimes invades nearby suburbs. Like the "wild man," the big cat has never been captured or killed. The Regional Park Service even has a name for him: "The Black Mountain Lion of Devil's Hole," after a region on Diablo's north end where he's most often seen. (We'll meet more of these elusive phantom felines later in the book.)

Directions: Take the Diablo Road exit on Highway 680 five miles to the park entrance. From there, it's an eight-mile drive to the peak's 3,849-foot summit.

Oakland Hills A large, ancient and cryptic series of stone structures line the hilltops here, just yards above the East Bay's hillside parks and homes.

They're a seven-mile-long broken stretch of stone barriers known as the Oakland Walls. Though they're concentrated in the hills above Berkeley and Oakland, wall sections have been found as far south as Mission Peak near Fremont.

The walls are from two to five feet in height, average about three feet in width, and are made of basalt boulders weighing up to one ton and carefully fitted together. Some sections run for only a few feet, others are hundreds of yards long. Most start and end without purpose or direction. No one—archeologists, historians or residents—seems to know who built them, or when.

It is known that they're very old. Early ranchers always explained them away as the work of "the Mexicans," "the Spanish," or others, since the structures had been on the land long before it came into their hands.

Researchers who have examined the walls' deeply sunk foundations, weathering and lichens, have estimated them to be at least several centuries old. Most historians doubt that the local Ohlones Indians built them, since the Ohlones were known to be peaceful, laid-back hunter-gatherers who would have balked at moving even one of the huge stones. The walls were obviously a massive, demanding project.

But the greatest mystery is their purpose. Though some of them might have served as fortifications, others, like the 100-yard stretch that runs up the southeastern slope of Round Top Mountain, would have been useless as defensive structures. They could not have served as effective pens or corrals, since there are no sections for enclosure or entry. Cattle grazing near long sections of the walls wander effortlessly around them.

Since archeologists and historians are puzzled by the walls, they've become an object of much wild speculation. Supermarket-tabloid theorists have identified the builders as everyone from shipwrecked ancient Chinese, to survivors of Atlantis, to extraterrestrial visitors.

One of the ancient, mysterious Oakland Walls.

The walls have also become a magnet for all sorts of East Bay eccentrics and cultists. When the author visited the wall section near Vollmer Peak above Berkeley, he discovered a ritualistic circle of stone cairns, obviously of recent construction, just down the slope. The cairns might be the work of one of the region's many occult or neo-pagan groups, who probably like the atmosphere of ancient mystery around the stone barriers, and hold rituals there much as their British cousins do at Stonehenge and Avebury.

But that atmosphere is in danger. Huge sections of the walls were carted away by builders in earlier years, and the remaining ones are endangered by developers and vandals. Like the Indian petroglyphs and cave drawings in other parts of California, the Oakland Walls need to be protected, so that future generations can puzzle over their unknown builders and inexplicable purpose.

Directions: The most easily accessible section of the Walls is 300 yards due north of Vollmer Peak, in Tilden Regional Park. Stop at the park headquarters on Wildcat Canyon Road and ask a ranger for a map and precise directions.

EL DORADO COUNTY

Coloma: *The Vineyard House* Robert Chalmers seemed to have it all. He was married to a beautiful, cultured woman; owned a huge, productive vineyard; held a seat in the state legislature; and had just completed a four-story mansion that he called "The Vineyard House."

Yet around 1878, just after the house had been built, Chalmers' mind and life took a bad turn. He became furtive and paranoid, started whispering nervously to himself, and began to visit a nearby cemetery so that he could lie in freshly dug graves.

Soon, Chalmers went completely insane, and his wife Louise had him chained up in the cellar. She visited him, some said, only to feed him and taunt him, standing just outside his reach.

After three years of this torment, Chalmers evidently became convinced that his wife was poisoning his food. He refused all edibles, and starved to death.

An unrelenting streak of bad luck later robbed Louise of her employees, her vintage and her real estate and savings. She ended up settling her debts by managing the building as a rooming house. As if this wasn't enough, her creditors turned the house's cellar into a temporary jail, and even hanged two men in front of the house.

After Louise's death in 1900, Vineyard House passed on to new owners, but none of them stayed for long. The house's residents all complained that eerie, untraceable sounds haunted the rooms. One owner even left suddenly and permanently in the middle of the night, refusing to say what had driven him from the house.

In 1956, the house was turned into an inn and restaurant. The cellar that once housed mad Robert Chalmers became the bar. But the haunting continued at full force.

Since the Vineyard House opened to the public, both employees and guests have heard rattling chains, rustling skirts, and heavy breathing in various rooms. Footsteps going down the cellar stairs have been heard when nobody stood on them. One of the owners saw a doorknob turned by an invisible hand. Something invisible also once tore apart a freshly made bed and made a humanlike impression in the rumpled sheets.

But a Sacramento couple staying at Vineyard House had the most dramatic experience of all. Late one night, they were awakened by revelers outside their room. Thinking that the celebrants were bar-closing drunks, the two stepped out, intending to tell off the noisemakers. The raucous party turned out to be three men in Victorian clothing who walked up the side stairway and then faded before the startled couple's eyes.

Directions: Take Highway 49 north to Coloma, and turn left at Cold Spring Road, just south of the Marshall Gold Discovery State Historic Park. The Vineyard House is about 0.3 miles up the road.

Folsom Lake This man-made lake in the Sierra foothills was (or is) home to a family of elusive alligators. From September 1957 to June 1958, visitors to the lake regularly saw these crocodilians swimming in the waters. Despite intense hunting, they were never killed or captured.

Folsom Lake is not the only inland California water that houses these erratic 'gators. Park rangers at Lafayette Reservoir west of Walnut Creek spotted an eight-foot alligator there in October 1975; a massive search failed to trap the beast. Back in 1930, a six-footer was seen in now-dry Tulare Lake Bed, and both the Kings and Feather rivers have been plagued by uncatchable crocodilians.

Usually these animals are explained away as "abandoned pets." This is unlikely, since "pet alligators" are actually caimans, smaller crocodilians that bear only a passing resemblance to their larger American cousins. Yet nobody's come up with a better explanation for why these 'gators keep popping up thousands of miles from their native habitat, or why they seem to elude captors like water-borne phantoms.

Lake Tahoe It only seems fitting that while other California inland waters house erratic, elusive alligators, the state's largest freshwater lake is home to something even bigger and more mysterious. Locals maintain that a large, unidentified, serpentlike creature lives in the 1500-foot depths of the lake, and usually appears around June in even-numbered years. Calling the creature "Tessie," in imitation of Loch Ness' "Nessie," they claim that the beast was first sighted back in the 19th century.

Tessie made headlines in the *San Francisco Chronicle* on July 12, 1984, when it reported that two women had seen the Lake Tahoe leviathan a month earlier. Tahoe City residents Patsy McKay and Diane Stavarakas were hiking above the west shore when they spotted the creature swimming in the lake.

McKay said the beast was about 17 feet long. She watched it closely and saw it surface three times "like a little submarine." Her companion said that the creature had a humped back, and seemed to surface in a whalelike, lethargic manner. She was also sure that it wasn't a diver, a log or a large ripple.

Two years earlier, a pair of off-duty Reno policemen had also taken a turn with Tessie. Officers Kris Beebe and Jerry Jones were water-skiing in the lake in June 1982, when an "unusually large" creature swam by them.

Tessie's never been photographed or left physical traces. Theorists have explained her as everything from a prehistoric giant fish, to a living dinosaur, to a strange paraphysical phantom. Needless to say, she still remains at large, swimming deep in the cold blue waters of the big mountain lake.

HUMBOLDT COUNTY

Bluff Creek This cliff-lined mountain stream, which flows through the Six Rivers National Forest wilderness, is the capital of Bigfoot Country.

By now, most Americans have heard of Bigfoot, the North American Abominable Snowman, usually from sleazy weekly tabloids or dubious TV documentaries. But for those of you unfamiliar with the stories and legends about this big beast, here's a summary of the facts:

Bigfoot, AKA Sasquatch, Omah, Skunk Ape, etc., is a wild, hairy, apelike creature who's been sighted sporadically in the forests and mountains of the continent since Indian times. He's between seven and eleven feet tall and, judging by the deeply imprinted giant tracks that gave him his most famous moniker, weighs several hundred pounds. Bigfoot is often accompanied by an evil odor that resembles the stench of garbage or rotten eggs. Both "male" and "female" Bigfeet have been reported, and in 1924, a Canadian miner named Albert Ostman claimed to have been kidnapped for a week by a British Columbian Bigfoot "family."

Nobody quite agrees on just what the hairy beasts are. Some researchers think Bigfoot is a primitive hominid species that retreated into North America's forests and swamps when modern men began occupying the continent many thousands of years ago. Others believe he's a surviving relative of *Gigantopithecus*, an extinct giant ape. A third faction suspects the Sasquatch is a miragelike phantom formed by unknown geophysical processes. And of course, there are the skeptics and debunkers, who write the whole phenomenon off as a product of overactive imaginations and sensationalistic journalism.

Indian tribes are usually the most reliable authorities on Bigfeet. Traditionally, they tend to regard the beasts as evil, and avoid them. They in turn generally avoid us. Unhappy with human incursions into their territories, Sasquatches have been known to vandalize backwoods construction sites and lob rocks at hunters who invade their domain. One "tribe" of Bigfeet even attacked five miners and destroyed their cabin near Washington state's Mount St. Helens many years ago.

These creatures have been spotted in every state of the U.S. save Rhode Island. Though they're usually seen in the back country of the Pacific Northwest, northern California has the highest number and concentration of sightings.

The "hot center" of Bigfoot Country in Northern California is Bluff Creek, which flows about 20 miles southward from the Siskiyou Mountains to the Klamath River. In the 1978 book *Sasquatch: The Apes Among Us,* veteran Bigfoot hunter John Green wrote that over 60 people had seen some 70 sets of tracks along the creek, and had spotted the beasts eight times. This made the mountain stream the most active area for Sasquatch in North America.

Though there had been rumors of mysterious giant footprints and "ape-men" in this land of steep, heavily forested coastal mountains all the way back to Gold Rush days, the real excitement began in 1958. That year, a timber road linking the then-primitive and untraversed Highway 96 with Highway 199 was being carved out of the uninhabited wilderness along Bluff Creek. Around late August, work crews noticed that something with

The famous Patterson film shows Bigfoot in action at Bluff Creek.

16-inch feet and a four-foot stride was leaving tracks around their camp at night.

A bulldozer operator named Jerry Crew became intrigued by the tracks and made a plaster cast of them. He took them to the *Humboldt Times,* told a reporter about the mystery animal and had his picture taken with the giant footprints. The story soon got onto the AP wire and was reprinted all over the country. The press appropriately dubbed the beast "Bigfoot" and the name stuck.

For years afterwards, road workers and loggers at Bluff Creek kept finding giant prints along the road and the creek bed. Some of them reported that they'd seen huge, hairy, manlike creatures loping around in the woods.

Most of the time, the Sasquatches fled from humans, but at night they emerged and scared crew members with their strength and growing aggressiveness. In the Laird Meadow region, Bigfeet toppled loaded trailers, overturned 450-pound barrels and threw a four-foot culvert into a canyon.

Many expeditions to capture the beast have been mounted, yet to this day, none have definitively proven that they exist. There are only plaster print-casts, eyewitness accounts, tapes of what purport to be a Bigfoot screaming eerily, and a couple of blurry photos. But there is the Patterson film.

The Patterson film is the most powerful evidence the Bigfoot supporters have. The 30 feet of 16mm color film, which show a large, apelike creature loping away from the cameraman. have been shown countless times in movies, TV documentaries and news programs to millions of people, and remain the best suggestion to date that big, hirsute monsters are wandering around northwestern California's wilderness. Not surprisingly, they were taken on Bluff Creek.

The film was shot by the late Roger Patterson, Bigfoot hunter and author of *Do Abominable Snowmen of America Really Exist?* In the early afternoon of October 20, 1967, he was out horseback riding with his friend Bob Gimlin at Bluff Creek. As they rounded a bend in the creek, the two men spotted a Sasquatch sitting calmly beside the water. Patterson's horse reared in fright, and he dismounted quickly, scrambling for the movie camera. Gimlin remained mounted, readying his rifle for action. Then Patterson quickly turned on his camera and ran about 80 feet towards the animal.

The camera caught a hairy biped with simian features, virtually no neck and pendulous breasts. Standing still for a moment, looking back at the camera, it then strode off into the brush, its long arms swinging at its sides. Right after the encounter, the men found 14-inch tracks where the beast had walked.

The Patterson film is highly controversial—dismissed as a clumsy fake by some and embraced as undeniable evidence by others. Most of the latter group maintain that the creature in the film is female, because of its distinctive breasts. *Argosy* magazine, the first to publish the film stills, dubbed the beast "the Adorable Woodswoman."

In the wake of the Patterson film's release, searchers have tried all manner of techniques to photograph, capture or kill the Hairy Ones. They've used every hunting technique imaginable, from baited traps, to infrared-scoped high-powered rifles, to helicopters. All to no avail. Bigfoot has eluded all captors, and though sightings in the area have tapered off, it's likely that he still roams freely along the steep banks of Bluff Creek—the most persistent and frustrating zoological mystery in the Western Hemisphere.

Directions: Bluff Creek is serviced by a National Forest campground and picnic area; they're about four miles north of the Highway 96-169 junction at Weitchpec. The old Bluff Creek Road was washed away years ago by flooding and landslides, but Fish Lake Road, just south of the Bluff Creek campground, penetrates the back country fairly deeply.

Serious Bigfoot hunters should consult the Sierra Club's excellent guide, *Hiking the Bigfoot Country*, before attempting to track Mr. and Ms. Sasquatch to their lairs.

Willow Creek A mountain hamlet at the junction of Highways 96 and 299, Willow Creek is the gateway to Bigfoot Country. The townspeople know it, and they've put themselves on the map with what must be the strangest town-square statue in California.

Standing in front of the Tourist Bureau office is a life-sized wooden sculpture of the Hairy One himself, carved by a local man, Jim McClarin, in honor of the area's most famous resident. It's a traditional first and last stop for Bigfoot hunters, who usually console their fruitless quests for the beast by shooting pictures of each other in front of his wooden replica.

Locals will usually tell visitors their favorite stories about the big brute; it seems as if everyone in town has either seen him or knows somebody who has. Store clerks, outfitters, gas station attendants and Hoopa Indians recount tales of huge footprints left in front yards, eerie humanlike screams echoing through the wilderness, and hairy, shambling animals caught in headlight beams at night.

Bigfoot hunts usually end at this life-sized statue in Willow Creek.

A lot of their stories might just be made up for the benefit of tourists, but there are still probably more sincere Bigfoot-believers per capita here than anywhere else in the state. To Willow Creek residents, he's their neighbor and friend, albeit a shy, retiring one.

LAKE COUNTY

Blue Lake *(13 mi E of Ukiah off Hwy 20)* In the fall of 1870, the residents of this little lake were terrorized by a huge animal that lived in its depths.

That November, the people of Blue Lake were having a lakeside picnic that featured a brass band. During the band's performance, the waters of the lake were suddenly disturbed, and a big, strange creature, apparently roused by the music, stuck its long neck above the lake surface and stared at the picnickers. A band member, telling the story to a *Russian River Flag* reporter, said that the creature resembled a "Chinese dragon."

Over the next few months, several locals reported seeing a 30-foot long "giant fish" swimming in the lake. It was said that fishermen there were terrified of the behemoth, and refused to row their boats into Blue Lake's deeper waters for fear of being attacked. Once again, the *Flag* sent a reporter to the lake to find out whether the monster really existed.

The reporter never did find out for sure, but he managed to interview

Blue Lake, the lair of a huge water monster.

residents who claimed that they had seen the monster. One man, an Irish immigrant named Michael O'Hara, told the journalist that he'd seen the creature from about 400 yards away, and described it as "at least twenty feet in length...(and) five or six feet around the body." Another resident said that he was trying to catch the beast with a venison-baited hook chained to a tree.

But by the summer of 1871, the creature was seen no more. Today, summer houses line the lake's southern shore, and fishermen and boaters ply its waters. The monster has yet to reappear.

Blue Lake is surrounded by privately owned land and steep bluffs; the best public access points are along Highway 20. Look for wide road shoulders and parked cars.

MARIN COUNTY

Mount Tamalpais Cone-shaped "Mount Tam" is the home of a bizarre creature that's either a two-footed black panther or a feline Bigfoot.

In July 1963, two campers were harassed here on three separate occasions by a five-foot-tall, tailless animal that looked like a mountain lion. According to camper Paul Conant, the creature's head "was close to its body, and below the shoulders it was very muscular. No ears could be seen." He said that the beast "chittered" back and forth with an unseen companion that hid in the bushes. Tracks found on the site indicated that the animal weighed about 200 pounds and walked on two feet.

Since then, there have been numerous sightings of both catlike Bigfoot creatures and bipedal "black panthers" around Tamalpais. Between 1958 and 1975, the *San Rafael Independent Journal* reported over 30 encounters with "panthers" in the region.

Both the pseudo-Bigfeet and the quasi-panthers are notorious for their brazen aggressiveness. On March 23, 1976, two Mill Valley policemen saw a hairy, two-legged beast climb an eight-foot wall in a residential district; the next day, a freshly killed deer was found on the spot. In March 1975, a "black panther" strolled casually through downtown Fairfax, stopping traffic along the busy Drake Highway. Other "panthers" have even chased and assaulted homeowners; this puzzles local naturalists, since such behavior is almost unknown among North America's shy big cats.

Whether these animals are two separate, unknown species or not hasn't been determined, for they have yet to be caught. Perhaps the Bigfoot/panther is a mutant subspecies, a strange new hybrid created to mystify the sophisticated suburbanites of Marin County.

Stinson Beach Eastern Marin County may be known for its bizarre Bigfoot/panther beasts, but this seaside town has been visited several times by one of the greatest legendary creatures of the earth.

On October 31, 1983, construction workers just south of town were idly watching the shoreline. Taking a break, they were looking for the nude sunbathers that frequent the lonely coast. But they saw something far more spectacular.

One man suddenly spotted a big animal swimming in the sea about a quarter-mile up the coast, and 100 yards offshore, and excitedly pointed it out. Crewman Mike Ratto then grabbed a pair of binoculars and trained them on the animal.

Ratto saw a dark, slim, 100-foot long serpentlike creature being followed by about 100 seabirds and two dozen sea lions. He later told a reporter from the *San Francisco Chronicle* that the sea serpent had "three bends, like humps, and they rose straight up." He said that the creature's head came up, looked around and then submerged. Finally, the animal's entire body disappeared below the water as it swam out to sea.

Over the next few days, more coastline residents sighted the leviathan. One witness said the beast was swimming at 45 to 50 miles an hour. Another said it had four humps, and "made 'Jaws' look like a baby."

Jack Swenson, a biologist at the Point Reyes Bird Observatory, told the *Chronicle* that there had been "periodic sightings" of huge mystery animals off the Marin coast for many years. Though Swenson felt that whales could be responsible for many of the accounts, he ventured that "there may be all sorts of prehistoric creatures swimming out there that we know nothing about."

MERCED COUNTY

Castle Air Force Base Museum If buildings wracked by war and violence sometimes become haunted, then perhaps vehicles can be as well. An old World War II B-29 bomber in the base museum here should serve as Exhibit A in this proposition.

The four-engine B-29 Superfortress (the same type of aircraft that A-bombed Hiroshima) is named the *Raz' n Hell*, and it's been doing just that since the day it was picked for restoration. Air Force Sergeant Ricky Davis, who helped restore the battered old warbird, said that when he first saw it lying in a heap at China Lake, a heavy pressure bulkhead hatch with broken hinges banged open and shut three times as if moved by a powerful, invisible hand.

Since then, he told a *San Francisco Chronicle* reporter, he's had a strange feeling of being watched while working on the plane. Though he doesn't believe in ghosts, Sgt. Davis says that "a lot of things have happened on that plane, but nobody believes it."

Second Lieutenant Doug DeWitt, curator of the museum, also believes that "something unusual is happening" aboard the *Raz'n Hell*. He says that he's seen a "solid shadow" moving around in the cockpit on several occasions.

Other airmen working in and around the craft have seen unexplained "things" moving in the empty cockpit. Once, two master sergeants swore they saw the plane's landing lights flash on, even though it has no power system and no bulbs in the light sockets. A reporter said that there were unexplained power outages and battery failures around the building the night he came to investigate the *Raz'n Hell*.

Researchers looking into the plane's history to identify the ghostly presence have been frustrated. The *Raz'n Hell* is a museum reconstruction made up of parts from several junked B-29s. Perhaps one of the parts— possibly something in the cockpit area—has a phantom crewman attached to it, a loyal airman who sticks with his plane even in death.

Directions: From Highway 99, take the Buhach Road exit, and follow the signs to the Castle AFB Museum. The museum is free, and open to the public from 10 to 4 every day.

MODOC COUNTY

Clear Lake California's past is violent and cruel, yet few of its regions can match sparsely populated northeastern California's bloody heritage. Here, Modoc Indians fought a long, savage and ultimately losing war against the white settlers who invaded their tribal homelands. Both sides suffered appalling casualties.

Clear Lake is said to be the scene of a particulary ugly incident. Back in 1850, the story goes, when a wagon train heading towards the gold fields was camped at the lakeshore one night, it was attacked by Indians. All of the settlers were killed, save for a young woman who escaped into the woods dressed only in a white nightgown. When she came back the next night, she attempted to bury her parents' bodies by the lake. Unfortunately, the Indians too, returned. They caught her and killed her.

Eventually, the Indians were driven from the area or killed, but one of their victims stayed on after death. Residents near Clear Lake began to whisper of a "woman in white" who haunted the lakeshore, wailing in ghastly, heart-rending tones. Her mere presence has been enough to banish would-be settlers. One night, a sheep rancher named McAuliffe camped at Clear Lake with his flock, and his sheep suddenly became agitated and stampeded for no apparent reason. As the animals bleated and scampered in terror, McAuliffe's normally brave and loyal sheepdog hid whimpering under the bedroll. Though the rancher himself saw and heard nothing, he left the region for good the next day.

Another sheepman named Connors heard McAuliffe's story and scoffed at it. He took his sheep down to the lake, boasting loudly that no ghost could scare him. Sure enough, that night Connors saw the woman in white walking along the shoreline and heard her wailing lamentably. His frightened sheep scattered just as his predecessor's had, and the now-humbled rancher gave the lake a wide berth afterwards.

Directions: From Newell, take Highway 139 about 16 miles south to Clear Lake Road. Turn left, and drive about 10 miles. The lake is now a protected National Wildlife Refuge, so be sure to inquire locally about visiting regulations.

Petroglyph Point This volcanic cone of rock, rising above the surrounding farmlands, is covered with petroglyphs: abstract shapes, animal figures and human outlines pecked into the rock about seven feet above the ground. Extending for hundreds of feet, the petroglyphs are fenced off to protect them from vandals, but can easily be seen from the ground.

Their age, origin and meaning are a mystery. Though they're attributed to the Modoc Indians, other theories abound. Perhaps the most colorful one is occult writer Harve Lewis' claim that refugees from the lost continent of Lemuria made them. (Lemuria was a legendary lost continent that allegedly sank into the Pacific about 15,000 years ago; for more details, see **SISKIYOU COUNTY: Mount Shasta**). Lewis was obsessed with the idea that the Lemurians were the common ancestors of both the local Indians and the Classical civilizations, and insisted that many Modoc words and place names were almost identical to the equivalent Greek and Latin words!

Directions: From Stronghold, drive south on Highway 139 towards Newell, and watch for the "Petroglyph Point" turnoff sign on your right. Take the turnoff and drive 3 miles to the Point.

Hundreds of cryptic symbols cover Petroglyph Point.

MONO COUNTY

Bodie A century ago, this mining town nestled high in the mountains above Mono Lake was synonymous with everything Wild about the West. The "Badman from Bodie" was a frontier archetype, a mean hombre hailing from a town infamous for its endless gambling, gunfights, robberies and killings.

Today, Bodie is a State Historic Park, and its unrestored buildings are mostly still standing, if slowly crumbling. The Park Service maintains the buildings in a state of "arrested decay," meaning they won't be allowed to collapse, but won't be restored, either. Appropriately enough, this "ghost town" is home to a ghost.

Ironically, the specter is not one of the legendary bad men. She's yet another "woman in white" who haunts the decaying but lovely little graveyard overlooking the town. Witnesses say she usually appears around the late afternoon and hangs suspended in midair above one man's gravestone, knitting. No one knows who she is or why she persists in her task, although it's been guessed that she's the mother, sister or wife of the man buried there.

Directions: Take Highway 395 north from Bishop, turn east on to Highway 270 and drive 15 miles to Bodie. Note: Highway 270 is closed during the winter.

SAN FRANCISCO CITY AND COUNTY

Alcatraz For 29 years, this 12-acre islet in San Francisco Bay was "the Rock," America's toughest and most secure prison. Virtually escape-proof, Alcatraz was the last stop in the federal penitentiary system for convicted mob kingpins, hardened serial killers and recaptured escape artists. Such infamous American criminals as Al Capone, Alvin "Creepy" Karpis, "Machine Gun" Kelly, and Robert "Birdman" Stroud were incarcerated behind its thick walls.

They and other inmates on the Rock served the hardest time in America. Alcatraz's prisoners were confined in four-by-eight cells, and given only food, clothes, a weekly shower and minimal medical attention. Rule infractions meant confinement in the "Hole," one of four tiny, lightless cells furnished only with straw mattresses; there naked, starving inmates were regularly beaten. Some men went insane or died after months-long stays in the Hole.

Despite Alcatraz's maximum-security environment, violence and rebellion often broke out behind the prison walls. Suicides and murder were common on the Rock, and one escape attempt in May 1946 ended in a bloody riot and siege that cost the lives of three inmates and three guards.

From 1934 to 1963, when it closed as a prison, the Rock was home to hundreds of violent, desperate men, and the scene of unimaginable brutality and lunacy. This made it fertile ground for future hauntings. Today, Alcatraz is part of Golden Gate National Recreation Area, and the island is filled with ghosts.

Most of the weird phenomena happen around areas associated with the prison's worst tragedies. There's the haunted Block C utility corridor, where the three inmates were killed in the 1946 uprising. In 1976, a night watchman heard a strange "clanging" sound in the empty corridor, which stopped when he opened the door to the corridor. When he closed the door, it resumed.

Other National Park Service employees have heard ghostly voices coming from the hospital wards, where maimed and insane prisoners were confined. Screams, running footsteps and a "crashing" sound have also been heard on Cell Blocks A and B. The shower stall, the scene of at least one murder, is also reported to be haunted.

Most Alcatraz aficionados agree that the single eeriest place on the island is Cell 14-D, one of the Hole cells. It's always cold in 14-D, colder than the other Hole cells, even when the temperature in the blocks is in the 70s. Guides and rangers say that there's a disturbing "intensity" that they feel in the cell, which is strongest in the corner where the naked, broken inmates huddled.

Cell 14-D's best-known occupant was would-be escapee Rufe McCain, who was kept there for *three years and two months* as punishment. Eleven days after emerging from the cell, McCain stabbed a fellow inmate to death. He was then tried for murder, but escaped conviction when the jury decided the living hell of 14-D had destroyed its occupant's mind, body and spirit.

Alcatraz, now part of the Golden Gate National Recreation Area, is open to the public. Tours depart regularly from Pier 41, Fisherman's Wharf, San Francisco; phone (415) 546-2805 to make the required reservations.

Bush and Octavia Street: *Site of Mammie Pleasant's House* In a town famed for its eccentrics, poseurs and unorthodox power-brokers, Mary E. Pleasant, better known to friend and foe as Mammie Pleasant, dwarfs most of her competition. In the anarchic, highly charged atmosphere of 19th-century San Francisco, this voodoo-wielding ex-slave became one of the city's most powerful and notorious citizens.

When she arrived in gold-crazed San Francisco in 1848, Mary Ellen "Mammie" Pleasant had been a slave, a housekeeper and hostess in upper-class Boston, the wife to a rich abolitionist who financed John Brown's Harpers Ferry raid, and a student of New Orleans' voodoo queen Marie LaVeau. Attractive, intelligent and ruthless, she was soon to make her mark on the City by the Bay.

Mammie initially took work as a well-paid cook and housekeeper, but soon grew bored and restless. Taking her cue from her old teacher Marie Laveau, Mammie recruited an army of informants among San Francisco's black population, who were given good jobs with Mammie's rich white friends in exchange for information and gossip about their employers.

Mammie soon knew about all the skeletons in the city's blue-blooded closets, and used the information for a wide variety of sleazy purposes. Depending on what the situation required, Mammie was at different turns a blackmailer, a soothsayer, an abortionist and a procurer. Favored clients were invited to her house for "voodoo rituals"—thinly masked booze-and-sex orgies that kept her black informants awed and her white customers entertained.

Mammie soon grew rich and powerful from her activities, but needed a front man to get into the big leagues. She found him in Thomas Bell, an investment clerk and old friend. Mammie had Bell handle her fortune, and despite his dire warnings about her investments, they all paid off handsomely. Fearing imprisonment and confiscation of her ill-gotten wealth, she had her fortune put in Bell's name, and he subsequently became one of the richest men in California. But all his strings were pulled by Mammie.

On her orders, Bell built a 30-room house at the corner of Bush and Octavia, complete with a secret passageway and a voodoo temple in the cellar. Here, she got him blind drunk one night, called in a minister, and had Bell married to a beautiful strumpet named Teresa, one of Mammie's many blackmail victims.

Mammie ran the couple's lives for many years and amassed a huge fortune through Bell, but around the mid-1880s, her power began to slip. Her methods of getting what she wanted became increasingly crude; often, she had opponents murdered. She ended up killing Bell himself after an argument about finances, pushing him down a long flight of stairs in the mansion on the night of October 16, 1892.

Teresa inherited most of Bell's fortune, and Mammie then turned her strange powers on the wealthy widow. But Teresa eventually broke free, and ordered the aging schemer out of the house. Mammie died penniless five years later, aged 91 years, certainly one of the most sinister and remarkable figures in San Francisco history. The Bush/Octavia mansion burned down in the 1920s, and a hospital occupies the site now.

And it's said that if you stand at the southwest corner of Bush and Octavia on one of San Francisco's fog-shrouded nights, and listen closely, you can still hear Mammie's ghost around the old eucalyptus trees, giggling and cackling, whimpering and moaning, plotting and cursing, still the Voodoo Queen of the City by the Bay.

The Golden Gate Another phantom from the city's colorful past haunts these waters when the thick white fog moves in. A derelict clipper from the days of sail power silently rides the Gate's rough currents, its crew long since gone to a watery mass grave.

Some say that the ship is the *Tennessee*, a clipper that went down here about a hundred years ago. Others are less certain, and just accept the craft as another anonymous member of the Pacific's great ghost-ship fleet.

The most famous sighting of the phantom clipper took place in December 1942. The *USS Kennison*, a destroyer on World War II Pacific duty, was plowing through heavy fog en route to San Francisco Harbor, when Torpedoman First Class Jack Cornelius suddenly called out for the deck watchman to look aft. The two then saw a derelict two-masted sailing ship nearly collide with the *Kennison*.

Cornelius and the watchman later testified that the ship had been visible for about half a minute and that its decks were deserted and its helm was unmanned. Another crewman, who had heard the clipper's sloshing and creaking below decks, backed up Cornelius' story. But the *Kennison's* radarman said that his instruments had registered nothing within miles of the destroyer.

Nob Hill If you're walking here along California Street between Powell and Jones, and a young, happy girl in an elaborate, Victorian-era white gown walks by and smiles at you, smile back. Then watch her very carefully. If you see traffic and pedestrians pass through her body, and if she disappears suddenly and completely, you've seen the Nob Hill Ghost.

She's commonly believed to be Flora Sommerton, a young woman who disappeared on the eve of her social debut in 1876. Flora's parents were pressuring her to marry a wealthy young man she despised, so rather than bend to their wishes, she took her Paris-made debutante gown and skipped town.

News of her disappearance made headlines across the nation, and a $250,000 reward for her return stood for 40 years. In 1926, she was finally located—dead, in Butte, Montana, where she had been known as Mrs. Butler and had worked as a housekeeper. According to police reports, her room was filled with newspaper accounts of her disappearance. She died wearing the same white dress that she'd last been seen in as Flora Sommerton 50 years earlier.

And ghost-hunters say she still walks in that gown, not in the form of an aged, lonely woman, but as a fresh-faced debutante, still trying to find the party that she missed over a century ago.

San Francisco Art Institute *(800 Chestnut Street)* There's something strange lurking in the bell tower of this Twenties Spanish-Colonial revival building.

In 1947, a student who was living there complained that ghostly footsteps walked up and down the tower stairs at night. Night-shift staff members also noticed odd things in the area, reporting that power tools and lights there frequently turned on by themselves.

Fifteen years later, a night watchman reported hearing a woman's laughter echoing through the tower and seeing a woman in a blue dress standing in the archway. When he went to investigate, she was gone.

The haunted tower at the San Francisco Art Institute.

By this time, many staff members and students had heard of the "haunted bell tower," though they didn't take the reports too seriously. The phenomena were annoying and perplexing, but they were largely laughed off by most of the Institute.

But nobody was laughing in 1968, when a major enlargement project focused on the tower began to go terribly wrong. Students working on the night-maintenance shift swore that something evil was living in the tower and wreaking havoc on their lives. The ghost was blamed for everything from a series of personal disasters that befell three night-crew members, to the unexplained sound of "chairs breaking" in the library late at night. Finally, the enlargement was completed months behind schedule after several expensive blunders and near-fatal accidents.

Several local psychics held a seance in the tower in October 1976, attempting to contact the ghost. Though they failed to reach any specific spirits, the seance members all agreed that a great feeling of creative frustration surrounded the tower, probably from the many budding artists that left their emotional residues on the building. One psychic said she saw a "lost graveyard"; the Institute is, in fact, built on the site of an old cemetery. But the exact identity of the tower ghost remains a mystery.

The tower is now closed due to fire regulations, but visitors can get near it by way of the adjacent school library.

SANTA CLARA COUNTY

Pacheco Pass *(on Highway 152, just W of the county line)* Take extreme care when seeing this mountain pass by car; it's one of the deadliest stretches of highway in California. Drivers usually blame the hazards on the winding two-lane road that links Highways 5 and 101 and bottlenecks the traffic going either way. But there may be a spookier explanation for the road's numerous accidents and near-misses.

Long before Los Angeles' freeway shootouts brought California's congested highways to world attention, Pacheco Pass had a reputation for provoking unexplained paranoia and violence from drivers. Highway patrolmen that cruised the pass had broken up many bumper-tagging wars and roadside fistfights, and ticketed countless kamikazelike drivers who tore through the heavy traffic. It seemed as if people were afraid of the pass and wanted to get out of it as quickly as possible, back to the safety of the big interstates.

Writing in *Haunted Houses and Wandering Ghosts of California*, Antoinette May said that she and other "sensitives" had experienced intense feelings of panic, menace and dread in the pass. They also had visions of marauding Indians and bloody battles between Hispanic and American settlers.

Ms. May wrote that after she had a traumatic experience in the pass, she looked into the area's history. Throughout most of the 19th century, Pacheco Pass had been the scene of tremendous violence between Native Californians and the various settlers. Highway robberies and public hangings were also rife there in the old days. The violence-ridden region might have received what ghosthunters call an "energy implant," a sort of negative emotional and spiritual residue left over from the bloodshed and tragedy that wracked the land.

Whether caused by ghosts, a curse, an "energy implant," or just the unfortunate linking of two huge freeways with such a narrow passage, the wild ride through Pacheco Pass is a grim reminder of the violent, dangerous emotions provoked by many of California's overcrowded highways.

San Jose: *Rosicrucian Park (on Park Ave. between Naglee and Randolph)*
In 1915, businessman and occultist Harve Spencer Lewis announced to the world that Pharaoh Akhenaton's secret society was now taking applications. The society was known as the Ancient and Mystical Order Rosae Crucis (AMORC), or "The Rosicrucians," and Lewis was its head.

AMORC claimed to have been founded by the apostate Akhenaton in ancient Egypt, and traced its heritage through the Renaissance-era "Rosicrucians" who antagonized the Church with their faith in science, personal enlightenment and a coming New Age. Many great men in history had allegedly been members of the secret society, and with the 20th century underway, the group's leaders had apparently decided it was time to go public and open their membership to the masses.

But rival "Rosicrucian" groups took a skeptical view of this history, and claimed that Lewis' AMORC had ripped off their credentials. Included among Lewis' competitors was the notorious English occultist Aleister Crowley, who said that Lewis was a poseur and con-man who had built AMORC out of a German "sex magic" cult.

But Lewis persisted, and AMORC thrived, dispensing its "ages-old wisdom" by mail to dues-paying members. Their ads still appear in countless magazines, proclaiming the secrets of "cosmic consciousness" possessed by the group. Since AMORC denies that it's a religious organization, it avoids the whole process of "converting" recruits—a major factor in its success.

AMORC's international headquarters occupies a city block-sized

Rosicrucian Park features Egyptian-style statues and buildings.

park in San Jose. All of the buildings have been designed to look like Old Kingdom shrines and temples, reflecting the Rosicrucian love of things ancient Egyptian. The park's elaborate fountains, tiled walkways, gardens and statues also faithfully evoke the Land of the Pharaohs.

Not surprisingly, the park's biggest public attraction is the Rosicrucian Egyptian Museum, the largest collection of ancient Egyptian relics in the Western U.S.. The museum displays relics, statuary, mummies and a life-sized replica of a rock tomb, along with several exhibits depicting daily life in ancient Egypt. Babylonian and Assyrian items are featured as well.

Next door, the Planetarium presents AMORC's vision of the universe and the future. The Theatre of the Sky features astronomical lectures and light shows in a large domed auditorium. Space-exploration exhibits in the lobby express the traditional Rosicrucian interest in science and technology updated to the age of moon landings and space stations.

And, closed to public eyes, there are the other grand Egyptian-style buildings. There's the Research Library, which houses thousands of rare books on mysticism and the occult. Rose-Croix University is here as well, along with the massive, secretive Supreme Temple.

But the real nerve center of Rosicrucianism is in the administrative buildings. Here, a computerized business operation reportedly processes several million pieces of mail every year. A permanent, full-time staff keeps track of members and groups in almost every nation on earth.

Thirty-five centuries after Akhenaton's reign, his San Jose-based Rosicrucians have become the Mystery School for the Global Village.

The Museum and Planetarium are open to the public every day except holidays; phone (408) 287-9171.

The Winchester Mystery House *(525 S. Winchester)* Despite the Disneylandesque atmosphere, the Winchester House is definitely worth a visit. Where else can you see a nine-acre, 160-room residence built solely to house ghosts?

The house was the creation of Sarah Winchester, wife of firearms baron William Wirt Winchester. Wealthy, attractive, and talented, Sarah was one of the bright lights of New Haven society, until both her husband and only child went to early graves.

Half-crazed with grief, Sarah sought help from a spiritualist. He told her that her loved ones had been taken by the multitude of restless spirits of men killed by the Winchester repeating rifle. They would turn on her as well, he said, unless she moved West and built a home big enough to

The 160-room Winchester Mystery House, a mansion built for ghosts.

house all of them. He also told Sarah that she must never stop building and expanding the house. If work stopped, she would die.

Sarah took the medium's advice. Coming to California in 1884, she bought an eight-room farmhouse on the outskirts of San Jose. There, she dedicated her $21 million inheritance and fat rifle-royalty checks to granting the spirits' wishes.

For the next 38 years, she and an army of artisans in her employ expanded, rebuilt and remodeled the house to hold the ghosts of Winchester rifle victims. The hammering and sawing never stopped at *chez* Winchester; Sarah's immense wealth and total obsession made sure that well-paid workmen were busy 24 hours a day, 365 days a year, Sundays and holidays included.

Sitting in a secret, blue-walled seance room deep in the house's interior, Mrs. Winchester held court with the spirits, whose constant demands for more room guaranteed an ever-changing floor plan. Balconies, fireplaces, rooms and whole wings sprouted up from nowhere like fungi. Barns were engulfed and observation towers blocked by the unplanned, uncontrolled growth. Mrs. Winchester made sure her busy staff got all the spirits' latest instructions; a primitive intercom system linked by miles of copper wire sent messages around the house.

The House that Fear Built grew to immense proportions. At the end of the four-decade construction binge, the Winchester House contained 160 rooms, 47 fireplaces, 9 kitchens, 10,000 windows and 2,000 doors.

Sarah designed most of the features herself, and some of the additions and improvements reflected her own bizarre intuitions and fears. Numerous secret passageways were hidden in the walls. Doors opened onto nonexistent closets, blank walls or three-story drops. Corridors tapered from normal width down to inches-wide crawlspaces. Stairways led nowhere, undulated like roller coasters, or compressed 42 steps into a nine-foot climb with two-inch-high rises. It was said that she installed these strange features to thwart the many evil spirits who arrived at the house courtesy of the Winchester '74 rifle.

A recurring motif throughout the house was the number 13. Believing that the number had powerful occult significance, Mrs. Winchester included it in such house fixtures as the 13-pane windows, the 13-paneled doors, 13-hole drains, 13-globe chandeliers and 13-step stairways.

Sarah roamed all over the massive house and never slept in the same bedroom more than one night at a time. After the 1906 earthquake struck San Jose, it took servants almost an hour to find her in the house's recesses, trapped in a room by a blocked door. Terrified by the quake (she thought it was caused by the spirits), she moved temporarily onto a houseboat, but soon returned to her monstrous mansion.

There she remained until her death in 1922, aged 85. It's said that you can still see half-driven nails in some of the walls, marking where carpenters stopped work when they heard that Mrs. Winchester had joined her friends and tormentors in the spirit world.

The house is a natural magnet for psychic investigators, and such famed occult detectives as the legendary magician Harry Houdini have visited the house. Many seances have been held in the strange "blue room." Mediums have seen unearthly lights bobbing along the endless halls and have felt the presence of Mrs. Winchester's long-dead servants and workmen. Even Sarah herself has appeared posthumously in the earthquake-devastated Daisy bedroom and the ornate music room.

But one final, supreme irony hangs over the spirit-built house. Neither the psychics nor the countless tourists that tramp through the house every year have yet reported hearing, seeing or sensing the ghost of anyone felled by a Winchester rifle.

The Winchester Mystery House is open 9-5:30 daily during summer; times vary the rest of the year. Call (408) 247-2101 for schedule and admission information.

Sunnyvale: *The Toys-R-Us Store (130 E. El Camino)* This big store has been plagued by ghostly pranks and disruptions almost since its opening in 1970.

Employees said that they would arrive in the morning to find merchandise scattered all over the floor. Often they would be touched or grabbed from behind by something invisible. Women with long hair sometimes felt invisible fingers running through their tresses. Light switches and faucets would turn on and off by themselves.

Night shifts were the worst of all. On at least one occasion, the night manager heard heavy footsteps stomping around in the unoccupied storage room. Once, a disembodied voice screamed to be let out of the locked store.

The case attracted the attention of San Francisco ghost hunter Antoinette May. May, along with psychic Sylvia Brown and photographer Bill Tidwell went to the store one night in search of the phantom. She initially believed that the ghost was John Murphy, a 19th-century rancher who used to own the land that the store now occupies.

But during the seance, the spirit identified himself as Johnny Johnson. Johnson, according to old records, was a ranch hand who had come to California during the Gold Rush, Devastated by an unrequited love affair, he later contracted encephalitis, which destroyed his mind and gave him the nickname "Crazy Johnny." Johnny spent the rest of his years working as a hired hand on John Murphy's ranch, and died there in an accident.

In death as in life, Johnson seemed to be a harmless, pathetic figure. The store employees eventually excused his attention-getting pranks and became rather fond of their resident spook.

In 1980, the television show "That's Incredible" went to the Sunnyvale Toys-R-Us store, attempting to capture Johnny on film. Again, Brown and Tidwell were present, but Johnny didn't show for the TV cameras. Tidwell was similarly unsuccessful with regular film in his camera.

But Tidwell also took an infrared shot of the gathering that revealed a tall, thin figure standing where no living people stood, staring glumly at the floor. It could only be the ghost of depressed, demented Johnny.

SANTA CRUZ COUNTY

Santa Cruz One of the strangest creatures ever thrown up by the Pacific beached itself on a rocky shore two miles northwest of this coastal town back in 1925.

Two views of the "sea monster" that washed up near Santa Cruz in 1925.

Reports of the time didn't agree on the size of the dead, foul-smelling beast. It was given as anywhere from 30 to 50 feet long. Luckily, a photographer was on the site, and took clear pictures for posterity. The photos show a creature with a duck-billed head, a long, slender neck, and a body trunk that tapers off into a finlike appendage. Close-up pictures reveal what looks like an elephant leg on the animal's neck; one witness said that it had several pairs of these legs on its body, complete with ivory toenails! To the observer, the beast resembles nothing so much as a plesiosaurus: a finned aquatic dinosaur that supposedly died out 65 million years ago.

And that's just what naturalist E.L. Wallace, who inspected the carcass, pronounced it. Wallace said the animal was toothless, weak-boned, and probably a vegetarian swamp-dweller. He theorized that it had been preserved in glacial ice, which drifted south and gradually melted. The carcass was cast adrift, and it eventually washed up on the outskirts of Santa Cruz.

Finally, an "official" scientific examination was made. The verdict was that the monster wasn't a dinosaur, but a species of North Pacific beaked whale so rare that it possessed only a Latin name, *Berardius bairdi*. The whale was unknown outside of British Columbian waters.

This didn't quite close the book on the case. Numerous witnesses still maintained that the beast wasn't a whale or even a known sea creature. At any rate, it wasn't the last time giant, unidentified sea beasts visited the northern California coast (see **MARIN COUNTY: Stinson Beach**).

SISKIYOU COUNTY

Happy Camp This logging town, 40 miles west of Yreka on Highway 96, was the scene for one of the most frustrating incidents in all of Bigfoot lore.

Back in 1967, two girls had been walking along an old forest road near here, when they came upon a dead Sasquatch lying in the road. The creature's face and stomach had rotted away, but most of its body hair was still intact. The girls believed that the carcass was very solid and heavy, since one of them tried to turn it over with a stick, but it didn't budge.

Their story wasn't reported until 1971. By then, the girls were unable to retrace their steps to the exact site, much less relocate the carcass that would have proven once and for all that the giant animal exists.

Lava Beds National Monument An air of violence hangs over this park in the lonely northeast corner of California. The violence of geological forces, where volcanoes spewed gases and cinders over the land and carpeted it with acres of lava now hardened to solid rock. And human violence, in an ugly little chapter of the winning of the West.

The area had been the home of the Modoc Indians for centuries, but when settlers arrived in the 1850s, a bloody series of skirmishes erupted between Indians and whites. They culminated in 1872, when a group of renegade Modocs escaped confinement on a dismal, distant reservation and headed back to the Lava Beds. An Army patrol was sent out to capture the Indians and escort them back to the reservation, but the armed rebels drove them away.

Thus began the Modoc War. It pitted 52 Modoc guerrillas under one "Captain Jack" against a 1,000-man U.S. Army force. After six months of bloody combat that made headlines as far away as London, the Indians surrendered. Captain Jack was hanged, and the remaining Modocs were sent to a reservation in Oklahoma.

It's often been whispered that Captain Jack's curse hangs over the land. Rangers complain that otherwise smooth-running cars mysteriously conk out in the park with alarming regularity. (This happened to the author's own highly reliable automobile not far from Captain Jack's Stronghold, the lava bed where the Indian partisan holed up with his men.)

If the Indians departed Lava Beds with a curse, they also left behind

Some of Symbol Bridge Cave's ancient paintings.

some strange, striking examples of their rock art. Here are two of the best ones:

Fern Cave (in the park's NE section; ask for directions) This cave houses a peculiar, lone symbol on its wall: a crescent and a small circle. Several Southwestern Indian tribes also scrawled this symbol on rock art sites. Some archeologists believe it's a depiction of the Crab Nebula supernova, which exploded next to the crescent moon on the night of July 5, 1054.

Symbol Bridge Cave (1 mi N of the Visitor Center) In this open-ended volcanic tunnel, ancient peoples covered the walls with strange, symbolic inscriptions. Many of the designs bear an odd resemblance to medieval European alchemical figures.

Both caves are on park property and are open to the public, although Fern Cave requires a week's advance notice before visits. For reservations and information, call Monument headquarters at (916) 667-2282.

Mount Shasta No place in North America is the subject of as many occult legends and stories as this majestic, snow-capped dormant volcano. Rising 14,162 feet above sea level and visible for over 100 miles, the mountain has been famed in folklore and strange speculations from Indian times all the way to the present. Whole cults have grown up in its shadow.

Shasta's story ties in such unlikely elements as white-robed phantoms, the Lost Continent of Lemuria, underground cities, gold-bedecked tombs, and a host of the most colorful dreamers, holy men and prophets this side of Tibet.

Our tale begins in Indian times. Local tribes, who had always considered the mountain holy, had a legend about an invisible race of beings that dwelt on the mountain. The natives were so afraid of offending these spirits that it was taboo to climb the mountain above the timberline. One old Indian used to speak of how his father had approached the forbidden timberline and suddenly heard "the laughter of children" echoing across the deserted slopes.

Mount Shasta also figures in Hopi legend. These southwestern Indians said that thousands of years ago, a race of "Lizard People" built 13 underground cities along the Pacific Coast. One of these odd subterranean settlements was supposed to be beneath Shasta. The Lizard People might have survived here into modern times; in 1972, a San Jose resident hiking on the mountain swore he saw a "reptilian" humanoid in shirt and trousers walking along the slopes.   (They may have also burrowed under L.A.; see **SOUTHERN CALIFORNIA—LOS ANGELES COUNTY:**

Los Angeles: Downtown.)

When whites arrived in the region, they began to create their own legends about the strange peak. The first one came from Frederick Spencer Oliver, a teenager who lived just south of Shasta.

Oliver spent most of 1883 and 1884 dictating a book whose contents he claimed he received from an entity that called itself "Phylos the Tibetan." Titled *A Dweller on Two Planets*, the book was first published in 1886, and is still in print, a classic of what is now called "channeled" material.

Dweller is largely about Phylos' life on the continent of Lemuria, the Pacific equivalent of Atlantis. Lemuria is often mentioned in the writings of such occult sages as Helena Blavatsky and Rudolf Steiner, who claimed the "lost continent" had housed a highly advanced civilization. A massive cataclysm back around 12,500 BC destroyed the Lemurian world, they said, and the land sank beneath the Pacific. Some Lemurian sages escaped the disaster, then burrowed into the hollows of dead volcanos and into subterranean tunnels and lived on secretly into modern times.

Phylos had lived several lives in both Lemuria and Atlantis, as well as in more recent times. In one account, he revealed a strange secret about Shasta.

Incarnated as "Walter Pierson," a California gold miner, Phylos was reintroduced to his mystic heritage by Quong, a Chinese. Quong took him to one of Shasta's canyons, where a hidden tunnel led to the secret meeting hall of the mysterious "Lothinian Brotherhood" deep within the volcano. The hall and tunnel, Quong explained, were hollowed out of the rock by a strange, powerful force he called the *Vis Mortuus*.

Marveling at the vision of this hidden temple, Phylos described "the walls, polished as by jewelers, though excavated as by giants...ledges...exhibiting veinings of gold, of silver, of green copper ores, and maculations of precious stones...a refuge where whereof those who 'Seeing, see not,' can truly say:

'And no man knows..

'And no man saw it e'er.'"

But one man knew, and had seen such a secret tunnel there, or so he claimed. The man was J.C. Brown, a prospector who worked for the British Lord Cowdray Mining Company

Brown was near Mount Shasta in 1904 when he came upon a partly caved-in tunnel in a mountainside. After clearing the opening, he found himself standing in a long, narrow room whose walls were lined with tempered copper and decorated with shields and wall pieces.

Exploring further, Brown found more rooms filled with gold and copper treasures, many of them covered with strange, undecipherable hieroglyphics. The rooms' floors were littered with enormous human bones, the remains of a race of giants.

This already unlikely story takes a cryptic turn here. Instead of carting off any of this amazing treasure, Brown quietly returned to civilization, and kept the find secret. Little was heard of him for 30 years. Later on, it was found out that he spent these years studying legends about Lemuria and its peoples and traditions. Brown was especially interested in *los gigantes*, a legendary race of giants who had inhabited prehistoric North America.

Brown eventually resurfaced in Stockton, 30 years after his adventure in the Cascade Mountains. Now 79 years old and living off an unexplained private income, he met with a local newspaper editor and a museum curator and told them his odd story about the Lemurian treasure tunnel. They in turn introduced him to John C. Root, a retired printer and occult student. Root was fascinated with Brown's tale, and the two men organized an 80-man expedition determined to find the lost tunnel.

On the eve of the expedition's departure, the explorers assembled at Root's house, and Brown told them that he would have a "surprise" for them the next morning. And surprised they were when Brown failed to show up the following day. He was never seen or heard from again.

Police investigating the disappearance were puzzled by Brown's complete lack of motive for flying the coop. He'd never taken a cent from the explorers, and had always seemed totally sincere in his desire to find the treasure. The case remains unsolved, and the tunnel, if it ever existed outside of Brown's imagination, was never found.

Around the time Brown had been reading about lost continents and giant prehistoric men, another legend about Shasta and Lemurians was being born. Astronomer Edgar Lucin Larkin was in the Cascade Mountains, testing out a new telescope. When he trained it on Shasta, he was astounded to see three gold-domed marble temples on one of the slopes.

Larkin had never heard of the Lemurians or their secret city at Shasta, so he soon began to ask locals about the strange temples. Townspeople in Mount Shasta and Weed were only too happy to answer him, telling the astronomer many odd tales about the mountain's unearthly residents.

They claimed that tall, long-haired, white-robed people were sometimes seen around the mountain roads and paths. The odd beings wore headbands, they said, to cover the pineal "third eye" protruding from their foreheads. Sometimes the white-robed people appeared in local towns, furtively trading gold dust and nuggets for supplies. When townspeople tried to follow or photograph the beings, they would disappear into the shadows or simply fade into nothingness.

Rosicrucian author Harve Spencer Lewis wrote about them in his *Lemuria, the Lost Continent of the Pacific.* He said that these beings sometimes chased trespassers away from Shasta's eastern slope, a wilderness area reputed to be their stronghold. There, the white-clad phantoms held eerie midnight ceremonies, chanting as they stood encircled around a great blue-white fire that cast beams high into the clouds. Lewis also claimed that inexplicable light beams stalled cars along the region's roads, and that UFO-like "boats" often flew high in the skies over Shasta.

Lewis' book, written under the pen name of Wishar Cerve and published in 1931, became something of an occult classic. The Shasta legend was reaching a mass audience, and it was only a matter of time until the mountain generated its own homegrown cult.

It didn't take long. In 1934, another pseudonymous book appeared telling of mystic adventures at Shasta, though it was given in the main to recounting revelations of "the Great Central Sun" delivered via the "God Free Ray" of the King.

"Godfrey Ray King" was the pen name of G.W. Ballard, founder of the St. Germain Foundation and the author of *Unveiled Mysteries.* The book, he said, was written "in the embrace of the majestic, towering presence of Mt. Shasta...."

Hiking on the mountain one day in 1930, Ballard had stopped to drink at a mountain spring, when a young man approached him and gave him a creamy liquid to drink. The drink turned out to be the Elixir of Life itself, and it electrified Ballard. Physically and spiritually invigorated by the beverage, Ballard listened in rapt attention as the strange young man began to talk.

The stranger revealed himself as St. Germain, the greatest of occult prophets. After telling Ballard the great eternal Law of Life, the good saint ran him through a whole series of teachings and tests. Ballard eventually became St. Germain's special appointed messenger and revealed his teachings in *Unveiled Mysteries.*

Ballard also set up an organization known as the "I AM Youth Foundation" in the town of Mount Shasta. Initially, locals were suspicious and resentful of him and his brightly dressed, ascetic followers. But by 1955, feelings had softened enough so that 3,000 Shastanians attended an outdoor Christian pageant put on by I AM that culminated with the actor who portrayed Christ ascending to Heaven on a cleverly concealed elevator. The pageant was staged in the Quail Hill amphitheater every August for many years afterwards.

As more seekers of mystery and enlightenment came to Shasta, the strange yarns and legends multiplied. One tale emerged about a race of dwarves living inside the mountain, in the city of Yaktayvia, who possess magic bells that are sometimes heard ringing from above the timberline. Another story tells of a huge boulder called Sphinx Rock, on Shasta's south slope at around 11,000 feet, sculpted into a human form by persons unknown. Bigfoot has made a few appearances at Shasta as well; in 1963, a Sasquatch allegedly carried an injured hunter to safety just north of the mountain.

In recent years, the volcano's century-long reputation as a place of mystery and revelation has become stronger than ever. During the summer of 1987, when the "Harmonic Convergence" was organized as a world-wide event among "New Age" groups to mark the beginning of a new aeon of peace and enlightenment, Mount Shasta's snow-capped slopes appeared on television screens around the world. Aquarian prophets proclaimed the mountain as one of the planet's prime "power spots" and specified it for the great gathering.

And indeed, thousands showed up at Shasta on the big day, August 16, filling nearby campgrounds and motels and jamming roads. But despite all the meditating, praying, chanting and humming, not so much as one white-robed Lemurian sage showed up to greet the assembled masses. Perhaps these wise beings feel they've created enough mysteries, and are keeping to themselves for now.

SONOMA COUNTY

Bodega: *Charlene's Country Treasures (Bodega Rd. just past the Salmon Creek Bridge)* If this little Northern California town reminds you of rampaging blackbirds and seagulls, it's because Alfred Hitchcock's terrifying motion picture *The Birds* was filmed on location here.

The film was fictional, but equally uncanny real-life events have plagued Charlene Weber. She's the proprietor of Charlene's Country Treasures antique store, housed in the 110-year-old McCrea House.

Charlene, a diminutive, plain-speaking woman, says that when she bought the house in 1974, the former owners said that they hoped she liked ghosts. She thought nothing of the remark until one day when she was upstairs cleaning the empty house. Charlene heard what sounded like a zither being played in the front room, and felt "watched" by an unseen

Charlene's Country Treasures, the haunt of a ghostly sea captain.

presence in the hallway. On another occasion, when she and her husband were playing cards, they both heard the sound of tinkling bells in the house.

To this day, Charlene's never actually seen the ghost. But visitors, former residents and psychic investigators have spotted him. They say he wears Victorian clothes and looks a lot like Abe Lincoln. Sometimes he's seen wearing a naval uniform and pacing silently around the house. At other times he's been sighted bending over what looks like a child's bed.

According to local history, a chronically ill child was kept in the house around the turn of the century. The man's identity is unknown, but when psychic Sylvia Brown held a seance at the house one night, he told her that he was a sea captain who had died there. And he angrily insisted that the house still belongs to him.

Charlene's shop and private antique museum are open to the public on weekends from 9-5, and on weekdays by appointment. Call (707) 876-3104 for more information.

TRINITY COUNTY

Trinity Alps Wilderness Though this rugged expanse of virgin pine forest and razorback mountain ridges is the southern flank of Bigfoot Country, the Hairy One takes second billing among monsters here. The most famous backwoods behemoth in the Trinity Alps is a leftover from the Age of Dinosaurs.

Since the early 1900s, prospectors and others who braved this rough country have seen giant salamanders living in ponds and subterranean streams. The creatures are enormous, between six and eight feet in length. Though five-footers have been found in similar terrain in Japan, nobody's yet brought one of Trinity's titans back to civilization.

Animal trainer Vern Harden came close in 1960. Harden and a companion caught one of the big brutes with a shark hook, and held onto the slippery amphibian long enough to measure it as 8'4" long. An approaching storm forced them to abandon their catch, though, and nobody since then has gotten their hands on one of the huge beasts.

Scientists who scoff at Bigfoot stories have been much more open-minded about the salamanders' existence. This is probably because the monster amphibians' Japanese cousin is officially recognized, classified as genus *Megalobatrachus*. They are believed to have once ranged all over the earth, but like so many other species, they vanished, leaving only pockets of their kind in Japan...and possibly in Trinity County, California.

Many determined explorers have searched the Trinity back country for the creatures. And enough of them have seen the loglike monsters lazing around caves and ponds to give the beasts credibility in zoological circles. So it seems only a matter of time until some tough, persistent herpetologist drags one back to a zoo or museum.

The salamanders have most often been seen in the region between the Pony Buttes and Limestone Ridge, about 25 miles northwest of Weaverville. This is some of the roughest wilderness country in North America; anyone coming here in search of the mammoth amphibians should hike in with an experienced guide and have reliable wilderness-survival skills.

TUOLOMNE COUNTY

Jamestown: *The Willow Hotel (corner of Main and Willow)* The Willow Hotel is actually a restaurant and bar; the hotel part burned to the ground in 1975 in one of the unexplained fires that have struck the building since the 19th century.

Employees, ghost hunters and others have blamed the puzzling blazes on malevolent spirits lurking around the site. But nobody's quite sure why the 126-year-old building is a target for ghostly arsonists.

The location does have a violent, tragic past. Before the hotel existed, a mine shaft that ran under the site caved in and killed 23 miners. The hotel

Jamestown's Willow Hotel is plagued by ghosts and unexplained fires.

bar was the scene of at least three violent deaths in frontier days, and it's said that a lynching mob hanged a man in his own room at the Willow.

Psychic investigator Nick Nocerino believes that the most likely cause of the chronic fires was the Jamestown fire of 1896. In that awful holocaust, the town had no water to fight the fire, so locals used dynamite to stifle the flames. Most of the town was blown up to save the Willow, and this, says Nocerino, might have angered spirits of people killed in the blaze and explosions.

Employees at the Willow say they've seen various apparitions in the building. There's a furtive little old man who wanders the halls. A mustachioed, black-suited gambler bellies up to the bar on occasion, only to disappear when served. The room where the hanging allegedly took place was the 1975 fire's flash point; witnesses claimed they saw dark "figures" flitting among the flames there.

Nick Nocerino contacted nine different spirits in October 1978 when he performed an exorcism of the building. He was able to get rid of six of them, he said, but he feared that the other three would be back to burn the hotel again, and immolate another building as well.

Nocerino's prediction came true. On July 20, 1985, yet another mystery blaze burned down the hotel annex, a barber shop, a jewelry store and a food market. The fire made headlines in the *San Francisco*

Chronicle, and for a week afterwards, the bar's phone rang off the hook with calls from strangers as far away as Hawaii and New York asking about the ill-starred building and its pyromaniacal spirits.

We can only hope that the unexplained fires have run their course, and that the old restaurant will be spared another immolation at the hands of Jamestown's vengeful spirits.

II. Central California

Fresno: *St. John's Cathedral (2814 Mariposa)* Elderly parishioners here still recall the days when this massive brick church was haunted by a ghostly nun.

A Sister Irenita, who had taught at St. John's School, died here in August 1931. Instead of moving on to a well-deserved rest, her spirit continued to walk the school corridors for years afterwards. Girls boarding at the academy were frightened by the ghostly nun's nightly appearances and footsteps in the hallways. Nuns said that they could sometimes feel Sister Irenita's trailing habit sweep by them when they assembled in the church.

After five years of haunting St. John's, Sister Irenita addressed the living for the first, and seemingly last, time. One day in 1936, her disembodied voice told one parishioner, "Please tell Monsignor Crowley to say the Mass for me that he will receive a stipend for and I will be at rest." The message was passed on to Monsignor Crowley, and he dutifully filled the dead nun's request.

Shortly thereafter, vandals broke open Sister Irenita's grave. When a Monsignor Cullen arrived to inspect the damages, he opened the coffin and found Sister Irenita's corpse soft and perfectly preserved, though she had

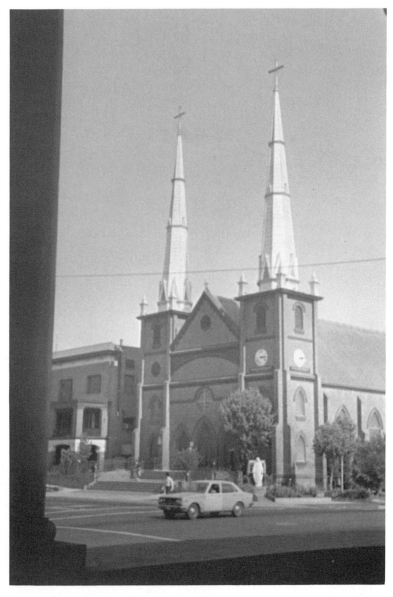

Fresno's St. John's Cathedral, scene of a bizarre haunting in the 1930s.

been buried for five years and a tree root had grown through the coffin. After this incident, Sister Irenita was seen no more. Nobody knows why she haunted the church for five years, why she wouldn't stop until a Mass was said, why her grave was opened, or why her body didn't decay.

INYO COUNTY

Coso Mountains On February 13, 1961, three rock hunters here made one of the strangest and most inexplicable archeological finds in California history.

The three picked up a brown rock near the top of an unnamed 4,300-foot peak 12 miles southeast of Olancha. Thinking it was a geode, they took it home, and almost ruined a diamond sawblade when they tried to cut it open.

When they finally split the rock, the real mystery began. Lodged inside the shell of petrified clay was a cylindrical object made of steel, porcelain and copper. X-rays later revealed it as a primitive spark plug of a type used in pre-1940s gas engines. How it got there was a problem, since a geologist who examined the outer shell estimated it to be 500,000 years old.

The bizarre artifact defies easy explanation. The few who have tried at all say it's a clay-coated piece of mine-machinery debris; this is unlikely, since the "Coso geode" was found several miles from the nearest mine shafts. At any rate, clay concretion processes don't happen in dry, rocky desert regions like the Coso range.

The spark-plug-in-a-rock was on display for a while at the East California Museum in Independence, but it's now in private hands. Its owners have disallowed any further dismantling or examination of the strange relic.

For all we know, the spark plug might be a cosmic practical joke. Maybe unexplained forces snatched a random object from the Industrial Era, took it back to the early Pleistocene period, and dumped it in clay sediment that encased it, at a spot where rockhounds would be searching for geodes a half-million years later. The perpetrators must be having a good laugh at the expense of 20th-century humans.

Death Valley National Monument Perhaps Death Valley's name is what gives the land its sinister, otherworldly reputation. Certainly, the subzero elevation, the searing summer heat and the moonscape panoramas also lend themselves to the atmosphere of mystery that surrounds the park.

And of course there are the legends. Tales tell of rotting wagons and gingham dress-clad skeletons half-buried in the shifting sands, of the fabulously rich Lost Gunsight Mine and Breyfogle's elusive gold vein, and of Death Valley Scotty's outrageous adventures.

A more malignant mythology has taken hold, too, in the wake of mass-murderer Charles Manson's capture up here in 1969. Manson, who had been involved with some of Southern California's most sinister and evil cults, was searching Death Valley for a passageway to a legendary underground world, where he hoped to lead his followers after starting a cataclysmic race war. He thought he'd found it at Devil's Hole, a deep, water-filled cavern on the park's Nevada side, but was arrested before he could figure out how to get his gang of killer flower-children through several hundred feet of hot, salty water where two skin divers had drowned just a few years earlier.

Manson may have learned of the underground world from the story of Tom Wilson, a Cahroc Indian who was a Death Valley guide in the 1920s. Wilson said that when he was a boy, his grandfather told him he had found a tunnel that extended for miles beneath the valley. Walking its length, the man ended up at an underground chamber where a race of fair-skinned people dwelt.

Welcomed by these subterraneans, Wilson's grandfather lived with them for a while. The people spoke a strange foreign language, wore clothes made of a leatherlike substance and illuminated their home with a pale greenish-yellow light of unknown origin.

The Indian eventually resurfaced and returned to his people, who were understandably skeptical about his adventure. But Tom Wilson believed that the old man hadn't lied, and he spent the rest of his life searching for the entry to this underground world, convinced until his death in 1968 that it actually existed somewhere beneath Death Valley.

At one point, Wilson teamed up with a prospector named White, who claimed that he too had found strange underground dwellings in Death Valley. White had been exploring an abandoned mine in Wingate Pass when he fell into a hidden tunnel that led to a series of rooms.

The rooms were filled with leather-clad human mummies. Gold bars and other fabulous treasures were stacked in piles around them. There was a passageway leading beyond the rooms as well, lit by an eerie greenish-yellow light. But White dared not explore any further, fearful of what might lie beyond.

White visited the rooms three more times, once with his wife and once with another miner. But he was unable to locate the cavern later when accompanied by Tom Wilson and a group of archeologists, though they did find a curious dead-end tunnel into the solid rock. The area around Wingate Pass was eventually absorbed into the China Lake Naval Weapons Center, and is now closed to the public.

Two other mystery sites in Death Valley are still accessible to the public:

The Amargosa Mountains (in the SE corner of Death Valley) Years ago, a desert rat was driving through this range in his Jeep when he came to a group of boulders blocking the road. He parked his Jeep, found a narrow pass between the rocks and walked down into a sandy valley, where he saw about 30 wooden buildings half-covered by sand dunes.

Too big and elaborate to be miners' shacks, the structures were laid out like a planned community. The explorer went inside some of them and found wooden tables set for meals, brass candlesticks, cloth and even an empty picture frame on a wall. There were no human remains and no signs of violence or natural disaster.

No record exists explaining this settlement, and the unnamed explorer's story could very well be another wild-goose chase designed specifically for desert neophytes.

Racetrack Playa (in the NE corner of Death Valley, along Racetrack Rd.) This dry lakebed features one of the most peculiar unsolved geological mysteries in North America.

Rocks lying on the lakebed move silently and secretively across its surface, cutting furrows in the earth and leaving trails up to 1,200 feet long. The rocks, ranging in size from pebbles to 600-pound boulders, have never actually been seen moving, but careful record-keeping by rangers and researchers shows that some unknown process does indeed roll them over the alkaline flat.

The most popular theory says that high winds push the rocks across a thin film of ice formed by rainwater. However, this doesn't explain why some rock trails are zigzagged, while others are straight, curved, irregular or even full circles. Also, some formerly adjacent rocks have moved in completely opposite directions.

More adventurous theorists talk of unknown geophysical processes occurring beneath the lakebed, but they have yet to be identified, proven or explained.

Recently, an unnamed individual allegedly carted off some of the Racetrack Rocks for use in a rock garden. Whether the stones started rolling around his driveway wasn't reported.

Racetrack Playa can be reached by taking the North Highway to

One of Racetrack Playa's enigmatic "moving rocks".

Grapevine Ranger Station, then turning left and driving 28 miles up Racetrack Valley Road. Be sure to ask at the station about road and weather conditions; the road is unpaved and the Racetrack is many miles from civilization. **Caution:** Don't even *think* about coming out here in the summer.

Lone Pine: *Whitney Portal Road (W of town)* Here, in the shadow of Mount Whitney, lie the Alabama Hills, a fantastically-shaped series of sandstone cliffs and crags often used as the backdrop for Western movies. The setting is highly appropriate for Hollywood's frontier epics. In the late 1860s, the region was torn apart by battles between white settlers and Paiute Indians. The Army was called in, and its camp in the Alabama Hills, at what is now Whitney Portal Road, was attacked several times.

In the 1960s, a woman living on the road who had never heard of the region's bloody history, was preparing dinner one evening when she heard gunfire coming from the creek. Looking out the kitchen window, she saw a black man dressed as an Indian warrior; he glanced back at her for a moment, then shouldered his rifle and looked forward. Several Indian companions near him, crouching behind a fallen tree, fired their rifles and fell back to reload.

The battle raged on for about 15 minutes, yet not one bullet hit the woman's house. Then, all of a sudden, the Indians disappeared and the air was silent. The woman rushed to her neighbors' house with the story. They believed her, having heard similar stories about phantom skirmishes along the road.

Records show that the spot where the Indians stood had witnessed countless ambushes and firefights between natives and the U.S. Army. As for the spectral black Indian, he was probably one of the many ex-slaves who had joined the native tribes, preferring their way of life to that of the "civilized" whites.

KERN COUNTY

Fort Tejon State Historic Park *(3.5 mi N of Lebec, off I-5)* This restored fort was formerly the home of the First U.S. Dragoons, a tough Army outfit that maintained frontier-style law and order in the region from 1854 to 1864. Only a few of its original buildings still stand, and the historical park now houses a museum and hosts mock Civil War battles on weekends.

The big old oak at the northwest corner of the parade ground is the legendary Peter Le Beck oak. Here a French trapper by this name was

The ghosts of Civil War-era soldiers haunt Ft. Tejon.

killed by a bear on October 17, 1837. Le Beck was allegedly buried under the tree, and an inscription telling of his sad fate was carved into the oak by persons unknown.

Legend has it that when word of the impromptu burial reached women living at the fort many years later, Le Beck's body was dug up and reburied in hallowed ground. Since then, his ghost has haunted the fort, particularly around his old resting place under the tree.

Some people believe that the Fort Tejon ghost is not Le Beck at all, but a dragoon who died in the hospital that stood near the tree. Mediums feel that the old hospital site is a center of intense psychic disturbances. They also say that other places in the park have these negative "vibrations" attached to them. These include the officers' quarters, the orderlies' quarters and the mess hall site.

Whatever tragic and bloody events happened in these places have long since been lost to history.

Kelso Valley A deer wanders this lonely, windswept mountain valley 20 miles north of Mojave. He's a huge specimen, with a magnificent spread of antlers. Hunters that spot him usually can't believe their good luck, take aim, fire...and then curse wildly, for the bullets never find their target.

Since the 1930s, the best hunters in the state have tried to bag him. The deer has been shot at innumerable times, from all possible angles and ranges, with all manner of guns, and from both open and telescopic sights. But he remains at large.

He's been surrounded by parties of hunters in the canebrake, who search every square inch of brush for him, his tracks or even the broken branches a flesh-and-blood deer would make. He always disappears, leaving no trace of his passing.

The Phantom Deer of Kelso Valley is just another one of the Mojave's curious wraiths, who, like the desert itself, remain alive, wild and elusive, despite all human efforts to subdue them.

Directions: To get to Kelso Valley, take Highway 14 north from Mojave, and turn left at the Cantil post office onto Jawbone Canyon Road. Drive up the road about 18.5 miles until you get to the Kelso Valley Road junction. Kelso Valley Road runs 25 miles north, and connects with Highway 178 at its end.

MONTEREY COUNTY

Mission San Antonio de Padua One of California's more isolated missions, San Antonio de Padua has been home to a "headless horse-woman" for over a century.

Legends identify her as a unfaithful Indian woman who was decapitated by her enraged husband. The husband buried the body and the head in different places, and the woman is doomed to ride the country at night, searching for her lost head.

She was sighted several times in the 1970s by soldiers at Fort Hunter Liggett, which surrounds the mission. Three different men guarding remote posts at night saw the headless, mounted figure ride by, her long cape flowing behind her. One soldier ordered her to halt; when she kept riding, he drew his weapon, only to see her disappear into the thin night air. On another occasion, four MPs in a jeep chased the phantom rider across the reservation, but lost her in the wilderness.

There's also been at least one sighting, on the mission grounds themselves, of a ghostly hooded figure carrying a candle. His story is as yet unknown.

Directions: From Highway 101, take either the Jolon Road exit at King City, or the one at Bradley to Jolon. Turn onto Mission Road and follow the signs. The mission is open to the public Mon-Sat from 9-4:30, and Sun from 11-5. Phone (408) 385-4478.

Monterey This former capital of California is the site of several notable haunted houses:

Custom House (in Monterey State Historic Park, at Custom House Plaza)
California State Historic Landmark Number One, the Custom House is the oldest government building still standing in the state. It's also the subject of some curious legends.

Many years ago, when the building was a boarding house, residents reported some strange occurrences within the adobe walls. Coughing and rattling sounds were heard in the house, and a phantom black cat sometimes prowled the floors. There was also a ghost that hung around the southern portion of the house, near the storehouse tower.

A former boarder once thought she had met the tower ghost. It seems that when she lived there, she had recurring dreams about a man who had hidden a pot of gold coins somewhere in the house. The man in the dreams eventually told her that he had been killed along with his son when he wouldn't reveal the treasure's location. He also said that their bodies were buried beneath the tower stairs.

In her final dream, a skeleton appeared and pointed a bony finger at an upstairs room's wall, where a pot filled with gold coins was hidden. Despite a concerted search, neither the gold nor the bodies were recovered.

The Custom House is open to the public from 10-5 daily. Phone the State Historic Park at (408) 649-2836.

Royal Presidio Chapel (on Church Street) Also known as the San Carlos Cathedral, this small Catholic church was founded as a mission by Father Junipero Serra in 1770. The mission later moved to Carmel, and the church became the soldier's chapel at the Monterey Presidio. It has been in continuous use since 1795.

Along the way, it picked up the ghost of a priest who had served there from 1897 to the late 1920s. Though he's seen most often at the rectory building next door, he's also been blamed for the unexplained phenomena that plague the chapel.

In the church, ghostly candles have sometimes floated through the air. Heavy footsteps occasionally echo through the deserted building, bells have tolled at midnight, and books and papers have been moved by unseen hands.

Once, the departed father himself appeared. When a troubled woman came to pray in the pews, the ghostly priest appeared behind her, put his hand on her shoulder...and disappeared.

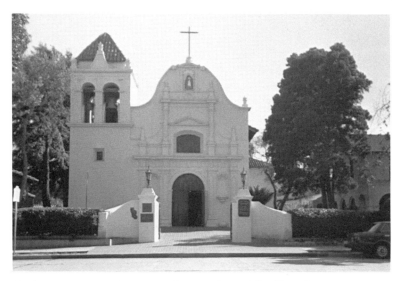

A phantom priest ministers at the Royal Presidio Chapel.

The chapel is open daily from 8-6. Phone (408) 373-2628.

Stevenson House (530 Houston St.) This 150-year-old adobe might have ended up as just another old Monterey house, had not a young Scottish writer named Robert Louis Stevenson lived here for several months in 1879. Stevenson had come to California to be near his beloved Fanny Osbourne, and had almost died on the journey. During his stay at the house, he was nursed back to health by friends. Eventually he recovered, married Miss Osbourne, and went on to become one of the greatest of popular novelists.

Stevenson moved on, but the "Woman in Black" has stayed. One of the most famous ghosts in California, she is thought to be the spirit of Mrs. Juan Girardin, the former owner of the house.

The year that Stevenson stayed there was a tragic one for Mrs. Girardin. First, her husband died. Then her two grandchildren fell deathly ill with typhoid. Working around the clock to save the children's lives, Mrs. Girardin herself caught the disease and died on December 21. Her grandchildren eventually recovered.

Tragic events that like these sometimes create ghosts, so it's not surprising that Mrs. Girardin came back after death. The "Woman in Black" has been seen more than once hovering worriedly over the

The "Woman in Black" haunts Monterey's Stevenson House.

children's bed in the nursery and walking the house's narrow halls.

The nursery, located in the southeast corner of the second floor, has been a focus for many strange activities. Dolls have been moved by unseen hands, and a toy Noah's ark once had its animals mysteriously rearranged.

Visitors have also reported the smell of carbolic acid (a common sickroom disinfectant) coming from the Stevenson bedroom, and have seen an empty rocking chair there rock slowly back and forth. Caretakers have opened the house to find books and other objects moved from room to room, and once a fresh-picked yellow rose appeared in a barred, locked chamber.

The house often instills strange, uneasy feelings in the visitors who tour it. Though most of them have never heard the ghost stories, they, rather than the caretakers and guides, see the "Woman in Black" most frequently. It seems as if she saves her appearances for the tourists.

The house is open every day except Wednesday, from 10-11 and 1-4; visitors must register for tours in advance. Phone the State Historic Park for information (see *Custom House* for the number).

Monterey Bay Home of Monterey's famed "purse seiner" sardine boats, Monterey Bay is known for producing creatures a lot stranger than the little silver fish that used to school here in the millions. Back in July 1874 and

February 1890, huge numbers of odd, unknown fish species ended up in fishermen's nets. The fish probably migrated to the bay by way of the deep submarine trench that lies just outside its mouth.

The trench coughed up something even weirder than mystery fish back in the 1930s. Around that time, Monterey fishermen complained that a huge, ugly animal with a long, thin body was pestering their boats. Nicknamed the "Old Man of Monterey Bay," the creature usually surfaced around early morning or late evening. It was estimated to be anywhere from 45 to 150 feet long, and about four feet wide. There were several humps along its grayish, mottled body. Most disturbing was the beast's face, which was described by some of the terrified fishermen to be almost humanlike in cast and expression. Others insisted it had the face of a crocodile or an elephant, leading one to suspect that several leviathans might have been living in the bay.

These creatures were seen throughout the Thirties and Forties, sometimes by every hand on a 12-man boat crew. The different beasts seemed to hang out in specific territories: the Salinas River mouth and Moss Landing's Elkhorn Slough were the haunts of the "elephant-faced" serpent, while the "crocodile-faced" creature staked out the Monterey-Pacific Grove waters, and the "human-faced" monster ranged south around Carmel. Reports of a "gorilla-faced" creature also came from Cape San Martin, where the beast was known to locals as "Bobo."

By about 1950, sightings had tapered off to almost zero, and the monsters went back to the deep, dark lair from which they came. (For an account of a sea monster that *didn't* get away, see **SANTA CRUZ COUNTY: Santa Cruz** in Part I.)

Santa Lucia Mountains These lovely, wild mountains that run southeast from Monterey all the way to San Luis Obispo are the home of the eerie "Dark Watchers."

The Watchers are black, humanlike phantoms who stand silhouetted against the sky on the Santa Lucias' ridges and peaks. Nobody knows who or what they are, where they came from or what they're doing in these mountains. Nevertheless, they've been seen many times over the years, seemingly staring into space from their hilltop posts.

The Dark Watchers were immortalized in different works by Monterey County's two greatest literary figures. Nobel prize-winning author John Steinbeck, in his short story "Flight," told of the hero seeing "a dark form against the sky, a man's figure standing on top of a rock" in the Santa Lucias. And the iconoclastic poet Robinson Jeffers wrote of the mountains' "forms that look human...but certainly are not human" in his poem, "Such Counsels You Gave to Me." Whether the two writers ever actually saw the dark phantoms, or were just drawing on the rich local lore, is not known. More recently, a local high school principal was on a hunting trip in the Santa Lucias when he spotted a dark figure in a hat and long cape, standing on a rock across the canyon and slowly surveying the surroundings. When the principal called out to the other hunters, the phantom vanished, and the man was left wondering.

SAN BENITO COUNTY

Hollister This is the epicenter of California Earthquake Country, a town sitting uneasily on top of the notorious San Andreas fault system. Seismologists and geologists have intensively scrutinized the area, especially in recent years, and they've noted a few peculiarities during the various quakes.

One was detected in the wake of a 5.2 temblor on November 28, 1974. Researchers had placed tiltmeters around the region to test if such instruments could be used to predict earthquakes. When they gathered data after the quake, they found that the tiltmeters near the quake's center had been showing disturbances as early as five weeks before the fact. A companion experiment done with magnetometers also showed anomalous magnetic field behavior in the area preceding the earthquake. The implications for using such instruments as early-warning systems are obvious and compelling, particularly in a state where the Big One always seems just around the corner.

Hollister is also known for "earthquake lights," bright flashes that light up the sky during temblors. Poultry rancher Reese Dooley saw these lights south of town in 1961, during two small earthquakes spaced less than three minutes apart. When the second tremor hit, he looked west and saw "a number of small, sequential flashes" light up a nearby hill.

The lights are thought to be caused by either air oscillation, or electricity generated by stressed quartz-bearing rock. They've been seen for centuries in Japan, and one ancient haiku described these strange illuminations:

The earth speaks softly to the mountain
Which trembles
And lights the sky.

SAN LUIS OBISPO COUNTY

Adelaida Cemetery One of California's many planned religious communities, Adelaida was a 19th-century Mennonite settlement nestled in the hills west of Paso Robles. Only the schoolhouse and cemetery remain today, and both figure in this tale of the supernatural.

Back in Adelaida's heyday, a woman who lived there lost her children to diphtheria. Overcome with grief, she visited the cemetery every Friday afterwards, placing flowers on their graves. But eventually her sorrow consumed her, and she died shortly thereafter.

Versions of the story don't agree on whether she hanged herself, took poison, or simply stopped eating and wasted away. Those who have investigated the accounts say that whatever the method, the suicide was probably hushed up so that the woman could receive a Christian burial next to her beloved children.

And she still visits the aged, weed-choked cemetery. Witnesses say she shows up on Friday nights between ten and midnight, wearing what looks like a white nightgown and moving silently among the old tombstones, yet another spirit held to earth by long-forgotten tragedies.

A tragic, white-clad spirit visits Adelaida Cemetery every Friday night.

Directions: From Paso Robles, drive 12.2 miles west on Mountain Spring Road; it turns into Adelaida Road. Turn right at Klau Mine Road and drive about 0.8 miles north. The cemetery gates will be on the right, near the junction at Chimney Road. Most of the Adelaida-era graves are on the crown of the hill.

Mission San Miguel *(in San Miguel, 8 mi. N of Paso Robles)* Tragic spirits haunt this peaceful mission, victims of one of the most gruesome incidents in the history of the California missions.

In 1844, the disused San Miguel was sold illegally by Mexican governor Pio Pico to an Englishman named John Reed. Reed reopened the adobe complex as an inn, and it thrived during the first days of the Gold Rush.

One day in 1848, a scurvy gang of English sailors staying at the inn overheard Reed brag about the treasure he'd hidden on the property. The brigands left later that day but, determined to get their hands on the loot, they snuck back at night.

Under cover of darkness, the sailors massacred Reed and his family, servants and guests, leaving a total of 13 bloody, mutilated bodies strewn about the adobe. The murderers then tore the grounds apart in a futile search for Reed's gold. Frustrated, they fled south and were eventually caught and hanged by a hastily formed posse.

Ever since then, San Miguel has been haunted. Early in this century, a ghostly woman in white was often seen wandering around the mission. She was believed to be the spirit of murdered Mrs. Reed.

Recently, Debbie Christenson, a psychic unaware of the Reed massacre, was taken on a tour of the grounds. She fell into a trance, and traumatically envisioned murder, stabbings, blood, and men, women and children being dumped into a mass grave. While Debbie relived the slaughter of the Reeds, a mysterious bleeding wound of unknown origin suddenly appeared on her back.

Old records show the massacre victims were buried in a common grave behind the church the day after they were killed. Ms. Christenson insisted that the dead could not rest until they were given a proper burial and a memorial was erected. At this point in history, that's unlikely to happen, and the victims of the brutal carnage will probably continue to haunt the quiet mission.

The mission is open daily from 9:30-4:30; phone (805) 467-3256.

SANTA BARBARA COUNTY

Chumash Painted Cave State Historic Park This little grotto in the side of a rocky ledge offers a rare display of the Chumash Indians' symbolic art. The cave walls are covered with wildly colorful figures. There are wheels with crownlike halos, circled crosses, Maltese-type tapered crosses and swastikas. Students of symbolism would tell us that these designs represent the sun, and that similar motifs can be found in ancient Celtic, Nordic, Chinese and East Indian art.

Other drawings depict horned animals and humans, as well as monstrous fantasy beasts. There are also more abstract multicolored blobs and stripes.

What the cave was used for is unknown. It might have been the temple of a sun-worshipping shamanic cult. Or it might have just been the studio of some prehistoric artist, leaving his cryptic works for posterity on the stone walls.

Directions: From Santa Barbara, take Highway 154 to the Painted Cave Road junction. Turn right, and drive two miles to the marker. The cave is protected from vandals by a grilled gate, but the designs are visible from outside in daylight. Open to the public free, every day.

Las Cruces Adobe It's now just a couple of decaying buildings, but Las Cruces ("the crosses") Adobe, situated in the windy Gaviota Pass, was once one of the wildest watering holes on the coast.

Ironically, Las Cruces entered history as hallowed grounds. After a savage battle here between Spaniards and Indians, padres gave the fallen natives Christian burials and marked their graves with the crosses that gave the site its name.

When the last of the crosses rotted away, a large adobe was built on the site. The building was used as a stage stop, saloon, and hotel.

Las Cruces Adobe later became a lively gambling hall, notorious far and wide. The adobe was especially infamous as a center of prostitution, and in time, the building was given over solely to that ancient profession. Eventually, the hotel-cum-bordello was abandoned.

And at night, when the wind howls through the pass and the moon rises over Gaviota Peak, Las Cruces' phantoms relive their lurid, tragic experiences. Two ghostly prostitutes, said to have been strangled here by an insane, sadistic customer, linger around the dark adobe. A third harlot, reportedly a suicide, sometimes joins them. There's also a tall gambler in a black frock coat, but nobody knows what violence or disaster anchors his

Ghostly gamblers and prostitutes linger around ruined Las Cruces Adobe.

spirit to Las Cruces.

Fortunately, Las Cruces Adobe is part of Gaviota State Park. The adobe and its ghosts are preserved, protected reminders of the wild, violent old days along El Camino Real.

Directions: From Highway 101, turn onto Highway 1, and drive 0.5 miles, exiting left onto San Julian Road. Turn left on San Julian, and drive 0.5 miles to the "Gaviota State Park—Las Cruces Adobe" marker on the left.

Lompoc Genesis 6:4 tells us, "There were giants in the earth in those days." That cryptic statement was literally true for a group of Mexican soldiers stationed here in 1833.

The soldiers were digging a powder-magazine pit on the old Lompock Rancho one day, when they unearthed a human skeleton. Not unusual, except that this skeleton, lying beneath a layer of cemented gravel, was 12 feet tall. The giant skeleton had double rows of teeth on its upper and lower jaws, and was surrounded by burial offerings: carved shells, huge stone axes and porphyry blocks covered with hieroglyphic symbols.

Local Indians heard of the find and panicked. They insisted that the skeleton was an evil omen, so the authorities, anxious to head off trouble with them, reburied the mammoth remains and the strange trinkets somewhere on the rancho.

Rancho Lompock's behemoth bones weren't unique. Giant skeletons surfaced all over America during 19th- and early 20th-century archeological and mining projects. Excavations at such places as Lovelock, Nevada, and the mound country in central Minnesota, yielded dozens of the oversized remains.

Indians in these areas were long familiar with the giants, and spoke of them with fear and hatred. They said that their distant ancestors had fought great, bloody wars to drive the Cyclopeans out of their territories.

Virtually all of the giant remains were lost or destroyed due to the sloppy record-keeping and storage practices of the time. Subsequently, orthodox archeologists have written off the many findings as hoaxes and the Indian legends as fantasy.

But we can't be too sure. Someday, a spade or earthmover delving the hills around Lompoc may again uncover a 12-foot, double-toothed confirmation of Genesis 6:4's words.

Mission La Purisima Concepcion *(4 mi NE of Lompoc on Hwy 246)*
These whitewashed adobes, not far from the old Lompock Rancho, comprise one of California's most haunted missions.

Trouble had followed La Purisima from the beginning. Founded in 1787, the mission was destroyed a quarter-century later by an earthquake. When rebuilt, it suffered a devastating string of disasters. Fires, floods, droughts, smallpox epidemics and Indian revolts all wracked La Purisima and its inhabitants.

In 1823, the death of the mission's dedicated pastor, Fray Mariano Payeras, spelled certain doom. Eleven years later, La Purisima was sold by the Mexican government. For a century, it lay abandoned and decaying.

The mission was restored in the late 1930s, and ghost stories have been told about it since. CCC workers who rebuilt the church found the skeletons of smallpox-stricken infants under the tile floor, and it's said that psychics can locate these improvised burial places today because "cold spots" hang over them.

There's also a ghostly gardener who's been seen tending the grounds with his hoe. The mission kitchen is allegedly haunted as well, by the ghost of a Don Vicente who was murdered there in the 1820s.

Strangest of all is Fray Mariano Payeras' church tomb, another center of "psychic disturbance." When the padre's body was exhumed here many years ago, it was missing its lower half. Fray Mariano's waist and legs were later discovered at Mission Santa Barbara, but nobody ever explained

Mission La Purisima's church contains many unexplained "cold spots".

why he was cut in half and buried in missions 60 miles apart.

One ghost story long attributed to the mission turned out to be a hoax. Legend had it that a phantom bandit on horseback guarded a treasure buried under a brick pillar here. Modern researchers found the tale to be a newspaper-invented hoax. It's just as well; Mission La Purisima seems to have enough real spooks to deal with without him.

The mission is open daily from 9-5; phone (805) 733-3713.

San Miguel Island This lonely, windswept isle is the westernmost of the Channel Islands. It's been the archipelago's strangest member ever since white men first laid eyes upon its barren shores.

Juan Rodriguez Cabrillo, Spanish explorer and official "discoverer" of California, is said to have landed on the island in October 1542, and named it La Posesion. While exploring the island around Cuyler Harbor, Cabrillo fell and broke his arm, and the jagged bone ripped right through the skin. Gangrene set in, and after its agonizing pain tortured Cabrillo for weeks, it killed him.

Legend has it that Cabrillo was buried in a lead coffin somewhere on the island, wearing his armor and clutching his jewel-encrusted sword. His coffin is the most famous of the island's reported treasure troves, but it has eluded all searchers.

Other treasure hunters seek submerged prizes at San Miguel. There's a Spanish galleon at the sea bottom off Point Bennett with a reputed $2 million in gold coins aboard. But would-be salvagers have been thwarted by the deadly currents there, sweeping walls of water that drown divers and dash salvage boats against jagged offshore rocks.

Yet treasure seekers have occasionally unearthed odd things on the island, though not of silver and gold. Stories are told of ancient, non-Indian human remains found here by visitors seeking buried booty. Once, a skeleton of a young woman was found at Crook Point with black nylon stockings still clinging to her leg bones; who she was and how she got there is anybody's guess.

Occultists claim that a vanished race of islanders left evil "spiritual residues" on the land, making San Miguel a locus for weirdness and tragedy. This may be the origin of the island's legendary curse against permanent settlers, though it's usually attributed to Cabrillo's last delirious utterances. Either way, the curse has claimed at least two men who tried to tame San Miguel.

One was a Captain Waters, who tried to establish his own kingdom on the island back in the 1890s. Saying that the Channel Islands were left out of the Treaty of Guadalupe Hidalgo, and therefore were not U.S. territory, he claimed them for himself. Waters then declared himself King of the Channel Islands, raised his middle finger in the general direction of Washington D.C., and sailed for his royal headquarters on San Miguel.

Soon, a naval gunship arrived to challenge the self-made monarch's claim. Landing at San Miguel, the sailors found Waters' sloop at anchor in Cuyler Harbor but no trace of him on the island. A month later, Waters' unmanned sloop was spotted drifting in the Santa Barbara Channel. Again, the island was searched, but Waters has never been found.

Another victim of San Miguel's jinx was Herbert C. Lester, a New York socialite who turned his back on civilization, and with his wife set up yet another "kingdom" on San Miguel in 1928.

King Herbert, as he called himself, and his spouse lived on the island peacefully enough for 14 years, raising two children during their stay. The royal family resided in a peculiar triangle-shaped "castle" that King Herbert made from native scrub pine and timbers salvaged from a wrecked ship.

But in 1942, the kingdom was designated a U.S. Navy bombing range. The government ordered Lester and his family to move back to war-torn 20th-century America. On June 19, 1942, the 54-year old would-be king, despondent at losing his island empire, shot himself. His wife and daughters buried him at Devil's Knoll, on the west end of Cuyler Harbor, and sailed back to the United States.

Part of King Herbert's triangular "castle" still stands. It's said that one of its walls still bears a single bullet hole, marking the place where the Curse of San Miguel claimed its most recent victim.

San Miguel Island is part of the Channel Islands National Park. Day trips to the island must be arranged in advance through park headquarters at 1867 Spinnaker Drive in Ventura. Call (805) 642-1393 for more information.

TULARE COUNTY

Lindcove Some of the best "hog wallow" land in California surrounds this town, 13 miles east of Visalia on Highway 198.

Hog wallows have nothing to do with pigs. They're actually little mounds of earth between one and six feet in height, and from 10 to 50 feet in diameter. They appear in California, Washington state, and the Southeast, and cover the earth by the thousands.

These hillocks are also known as "Mima mounds," after the Mima Plain in Washington state, where they occupy many square miles of land. In California's Central Valley region, the mounds are so numerous that a farm implement known as the "Fresno scraper" was invented specifically to level them.

Farmers may have regarded the mounds as nuisances to be flattened, but geologists have long been fascinated and perplexed by these peculiar earth pimples. They've dreamed up all manner of unlikely theories to explain them. Gophers have been suggested as the culprits, but the Lindcove mounds contain rocks far too big for rodents to lift. Others have believed the builders to be Indians, ants, water erosion, wind action, uprooted trees, underground springs, geothermal vents, and even prehistoric shovel-nosed sharks that scooped the ancient ocean bottom into neat little piles.

All of these theories have serious deficiencies, and no consensus exists on any of them among scientists. The mounds remain one of the great unsolved earth mysteries of America.

VENTURA COUNTY

Aliso Canyon *(6 mi W of Santa Paula)* At the end of this twisting mountain road lies the lair of one of California's most grotesque and frightening creatures: the Billiwack Monster.

The beast takes its name from the abandoned Billiwack Dairy, built in 1925 by August Rubel. Rubel sought to create an efficient, high-tech dairy, but he was ruined by the Depression. The dairy itself was abandoned in 1943.

Rubel mysteriously disappeared that same year while on a "secret mission" for the U.S. Army in North Africa. His activities and fate were

Artist's depiction of the grotesque "Billiwack Monster".

never revealed.

Soon after Rubel's disappearance, there came rumors of ghosts and monsters haunting the old dairy. People said that a huge, humanlike creature lurked around the ruins at night. It was described as being muscular and powerful, with gray hair covering its body, long talons on its fingers, and a horned, ramlike head. One witness said it had shining, feline yellow-green eyes. Its most dramatic appearance was back in 1964, when the beast terrified a group of boys hiking in the canyon. The incident made headlines all over California.

Through the years, the monster has made infrequent nocturnal appearances in Aliso Canyon. Much local speculation and lore involves the creature. Though many dismiss it as the creation of overactive juvenile imaginations (many of its witnesses have been teenagers), others are convinced the beast is real. It's been variously called a deformed Bigfoot, a mutant offspring of Rubel's breeding experiments, and a simple (if fantastic-appearing) ghost.

The latter explanation may be the most popular one. Recently, a local paper's poll asked Ventura residents who their favorite ghost was. Despite stiff competition from history-haunted Central California's many phantoms, the Billiwack Monster was the hands-down winner.

Camp Comfort County Park *(1.5 mi S of Ojai on Creek Road)* Another grotesque specter hangs out here at the Creek Road bridge. He's called Charman, and local-lore experts can't agree on whether he was a fire-fighter killed in the great brush blaze of 1948 or a motorist who perished in a fiery auto wreck.

Either way, the man burned to a crisp somewhere in the surrounding woods, and is doomed to haunt the road at night. Witnesses say he's horribly disfigured: peeling, charred flesh hangs from his skull, and he's barely clothed in seared, disheveled rags. Sometimes even the awful stench of burning flesh precedes him.

Charman is one of the region's more aggressive phantoms. He's said to hide in the dark woods, coming out to attack people walking the road at night. Back in the 1950s, he allegedly grabbed a young man and tore his jacket off; when the story made the newspapers, Creek Road was jammed with sightseers looking for the gruesome apparition.

The hideous spirit has picked up some ghostly friends along Creek Road in recent years. One is a phantom horsewoman usually seen on moonlit nights; she was killed while riding along this road. There's also a ghostly hitchhiker, a woman wearing a wedding dress

The hideous "Charman" lurks in the woods around Creek Road Bridge.

who thumbs rides from the living. She is just one of the many "phantom hitchhikers" who haunt America's highways and back roads; so commonly are they reported that they've become sort of an archetype in our folklore.

Yet another Creek Road spook is the "headless biker" who rides a big prewar motorcycle. In earlier years, he would almost certainly have been a "headless horseman." Perhaps such decapitated spirits are now spurning white chargers in favor of classic two-wheelers.

Conejo Valley *(1 mi NW of Newbury Park)* At least two of California's notorious "phantom panthers" roam this mountain valley.

The big cats have been sighted around here since the early Sixties, and have been the object of several major hunts since 1964. To this day, nobody's bagged one of the felines.

Ventura County sheriff's deputies thought they had one of the big cats cornered back on December 12, 1967. Workers at the county sewage treatment plant had spotted one of the panthers strutting around a nearby hillside, and had called the county sheriff's office, all the while keeping close eyes on the feline. When the deputies arrived, they sighted down the panther and drove their squad car straight at the beast. The deputies made a bad move, though, when they drove off the road onto what looked like a flat dirt field. The "field" turned out to be a dry crust covering a sewage pond, and as the car nose-dived into the stinking lake of filth, the panther turned tail and escaped.

The panther was seen several more times that month, once by a hunter who got trapped on a sheer mountain ledge while pursuing the cat. Like its Northern Californian cousins (see **CONTRA COSTA COUNTY: Mount Diablo; and MARIN COUNTY: Mount Tamalpais**), the feline is phantomlike and uncatchable. So many people have gotten into serious trouble while hunting the cats, that they're now thought of as evil omens and are usually left alone.

Grimes Canyon *(3 mi S of Fillmore on Hwy 23)* Peculiar geological processes shaped this rugged canyon on Oak Ridge's north side. Rocks lying in a 12-mile long, mile-wide belt here were melted into primordial plastic by white-hot spontaneous combustion deep beneath the surface.

The process, called combustion metamorphism, was probably touched off by decaying organic matter some time in the Ice Age. Temperatures reached 1,600 degrees Celsius, and the melted rock warped and layered the surrounding earth. The rock may still have been smoldering underground as recently as a century ago.

Grimes Canyon is one of several areas across the earth where non-volcanic forces have melted solid rock. Renegade geologists have eagerly tried to explain them as leftover "hot spots" from a fiery prehistoric cataclysm, but their theories have mostly been ignored by mainstream science.

Ventura: *The Olivas Adobe (4200 Olivas Park Drive)* Senora Teodora Olivas may still be hanging around this big hacienda almost a century after her death. The wife of cattle baron Don Raimundo and mother of their 22 children, she is believed to be the "dark lady" who appears in the kitchen and the living room, and whose ghostly footsteps are heard on the balcony.

Having to bear and raise that many *ninos* would be traumatic enough to make her want to haunt the living. But the legends point to one incident involving Senora Olivas that may have given her special reason to linger around the adobe.

In 1855, bandits raided the Olivas Adobe in search of the Don's treasure. While ransacking the house, the badmen tormented the residents, and one of them struck down Senora Olivas and ripped the gold earrings out of her earlobes. A posse later caught and hanged some of the bandits, but their loot was never recovered.

Legends tell of a ghostly "dark lady" and buried treasure at Olivas Adobe.

One story says that the raiders got away with about $75,000 in gold and buried it somewhere between Ventura and Santa Barbara. Nobody's yet found the hiding place.

Another account has an Indian servant frantically burying Don Raimundo's treasure box on the grounds while the Don distracted the bandits. When the Indian returned, the brigands killed him, and he took the buried gold's location to his grave.

So perhaps it's the still-lost chunk of the Olivas fortune that the Dark Lady of Olivas Adobe is searching for in her ghostly forays around the house.

Olivas Adobe is a State Historic Monument, and is open from 9-4 daily; phone (805) 654-7837.

III. Southern California

IMPERIAL COUNTY

Salton Sea Somewhere beneath the brackish, sub-sea level waters of this huge lake lies the rotting hulk of an ancient Spanish galleon. Or it might be hidden somewhere on the shore, its broken timbers and masts buried in the shifting sands. No one knows for sure, but the legend of the Lost Ship of the Desert has become one of the Southwest's most tantalizing tales.

How did a seagoing vessel beach itself a hundred miles inland? Legend has it that in the 16th century, what's now the Imperial Valley was then an inland sea, linked by passages through the flooded valley to the Colorado River and, from that, to the Gulf of California.

Spanish ships are said to have frequently sailed into this desert sea. Their navigators thought that California was an island surrounded by the Pacific, the then-unexplored San Francisco Bay, and this vanished body of water. Some maps of the period even showed California as an island, with a strait of water going through the Central Valley to the Mojave Desert.

One galleon was sailing up around what's now the Salton Sea, when it either hit a sandbar, or sank in a storm. Either way, it was left high and dry when a great earthquake hit, and drained the waters of the sea back to the Colorado River.

Indians, Spaniards, Mexicans and American prospectors all had stories about the great ship that they had seen lying in the Imperial Valley desert sands. Though geographers deny that the valley held water during the period of Spanish exploration and conquest, the myth refuses to die. Many men have been convinced that the ship really exists, and have searched the valley and the surrounding desert for the vessel. And one man actually claimed that he had found the ancient, landlocked craft.

He was Charley Clusker, a miner who led three expeditions to find the galleon back in 1870. A veteran of many desert and mountain adventures, Charley heard about the lost ship at age 60, got two men to bankroll an expedition and accompany him, and set off in search of the phantom craft.

The first attempt ended in failure, but Charley and three new companions headed into the desert again, and claimed they found the rotting hulk on this second try. The *San Bernardino Guardian*, following his adventures, placed the wreck "45 miles southwest of Dos Palmas Station," which would put it around the mouth of San Felipe Creek at the Salton Sea. The paper then printed some wild, exaggerated stories, describing the ship as 200 feet long, decorated with ornate crosses and filled with gold doubloons and pearls.

On the third expedition, Charley and a new crew loaded themselves down with picks, shovels and other salvage implements, and headed out towards the Salton Sink once more. But after a suspiciously long time, they reappeared in civilization empty-handed. They claimed that their animals had been worn out by the long, rough journey, and they were forced to turn back. This wasn't surprising, since Charley and his party approached the ship's supposed location from an unexplained detour that took them dozens of miles out of their way.

By this time, some commentators were getting very suspicious of Charley's claims. They hinted that he wasn't interested in finding the ship as much as he was in doing a little good old-fashioned prospecting on other people's money. Skeptics pointed out that Charley's trip-mates had paid for all of the expeditions, and said that he was approaching the "lost ship" from different angles so that he could cover as much new gold country as possible, courtesy of his mates' grubstakes.

To be fair, though, Charley did seem to be convinced of the ship's existence, truly believing that he had pinpointed the landlocked craft's location in what was then the dry, hard-bottomed Salton Sink. He and his associates probably gave up on the third trip when they found the ship, searched it, and found no treasure.

Eventually Charley moved on to chase other golden phantoms, and the Lost Ship of the Desert entered Western lore as an unsolved mystery.

The Salton Sink was flooded in a storm, and the area that Charley and his men searched in was submerged under several fathoms of water. Now the Salton Sea is slowly drying up, and the paths that the lost-ship hunters walked are exposed for the first time in decades. What strange, ancient artifacts might someday poke above the sinking surface can only be guessed at. Charley Clusker might yet be vindicated. (For an account of an even more fantastic Lost Desert Ship, see **SAN DIEGO COUNTY: Anza-Borrego State Park:** *Agua Caliente Springs*.)

LOS ANGELES COUNTY

Big Rock Canyon *(8 mi SE of Pearblossom on Big Rock Creek Rd.)* This rugged canyon on the San Gabriel Mountains' north slope is a sort of Bluff Creek South. The area is believed to be the home base of Southern California Sasquatches who have terrified hikers and homeowners in the San Gabriels and the Antelope Valley.

These creatures had been rumored to exist in the Southern California back country for many years. Indians told Spanish padres of the "hairy giants who supposedly live up certain dry arroyos." In 1876, white hunters spotted an apelike beast roaming the mountains near Warner's Ranch in San Diego County.

But Southern California's real Bigfoot epidemic hit in the mid-1960s. In 1966, newspaper reports told of a girl pawed by a seven-foot-tall, slime-covered beast in the Lytle Creek wash north of Fontana. A few weeks earlier, two boys hiking in the wash had seen "an ape in a tree" there. In 1965, two picnickers had been chased from their campfire by a nine- or ten-foot-tall, hairy creature on the north slope of the San Gorgonio Mountains. And way over in Quartz Hill, on the west end of the Antelope Valley, two young men told L.A. County sheriffs that they had seen a dark, giant biped silhouetted against the sky on a hill.

Such reports tantalized and perplexed Sasquatch hunters. They had previously concentrated their search for the Hairy One in the rugged forest wilderness of northwestern California, and it seemed incredible, and more than a little disturbing, that the big ape could be lurking on the outskirts of Los Angeles itself.

Hunters picked up the Southland Bigfoot trail in Big Rock Canyon in 1973. That year, huge apelike creatures were reported all over Antelope Valley. Frightened homeowners and frustrated lawmen were never able to capture any of the beasts, and believed that they hid out in the neighboring San Gabriel Mountains. Sasquatch expert Ken Coon hired a plane, flew over the mountains, saw forested, creek-fed Big Rock Canyon and guessed that the wild mountain valley was probably the Sasquatches' Los Angeles County lair.

And sure enough, Bigfoot turned up in Big Rock Canyon. On April 22, 1973, three young men from the San Fernando Valley, William Roemermann, Brian Goldojarb and Richard Engels, saw him there near the Sycamore Flats campground. Richard and Brian had been riding in the back of their pickup truck that night, at about 10 PM, when an 11-foot Sasquatch jumped out of the bushes and chased the truck for about 20 seconds, its long arms swinging in front of its chest.

The boys reported the incident to the sheriff's office in Lancaster and went straight back to Big Rock Canyon. There they located the spot where the big ape had appeared, and were amazed to find hundreds of huge footprints along the road, some of which they later preserved in plaster of Paris. These prints were especially odd, as they were three-toed. Normal Bigfoot tracks are five-toed.

Soon, hunters were scouring Big Rock Canyon for the three-toed Sasquatches, and more sightings and track-casts rolled in. Six months after the encounter at Sycamore Flats, something left 21-inch tracks with a 12-foot stride at South Fork campground. The behemoth that made them, perhaps fortunately, was nowhere in sight. He may have revealed himself the following month, though, when Bigfoot hunter Margaret Bailey saw a "huge figure" in the moonlight at Sycamore Flats.

Then came the inevitable tapering-off of reports. Once again, the hairy giants retreated from public view, and headed back to whatever strange twilight world they inhabit. They were seen one more time each in 1974, 1975 and 1976 around Big Rock campground at the top of the canyon. William Roemermann, who had become Big Rock Canyon's answer to Roger Patterson, made the last two sightings.

The author was told that Bigfoot was last seen in the region at Devil's Punchbowl County Park a few years ago, when two girls and their horses were scared senseless by an apelike monster. Since Devil's Punchbowl is just west of Big Rock Canyon, it's likely that the creatures are still dwelling in the area, and might make a comeback before too long.

Calabasas: *The Leonis Adobe (23537 Calabasas Road)* The husband-and-wife ghost team of Miguel and Espiritu Leonis haunts this restored adobe on the edge of the San Fernando Valley.

Miguel Leonis was a Basque immigrant who made his home here a century ago. One of the classic strong, silent Western ranchers, he was feared throughout Southern California for his dictatorial control of his massive ranch.

Leonis, a huge, powerful man who could throw a yearling 20 feet into a wagon, built his empire through persistence, craftiness and ruthlessness. At the height of his power, his ranch covered most of the western San Fernando Valley, and stretched south to the Pacific and west into Ventura County. It didn't matter to Leonis that much of this land was legally in the public domain; he merely hauled trespassers on the land to the city jail, and constantly sued rival claimants. Leonis' name can be found all over early Los Angeles court records.

When litigation didn't work for the big Basque, he resorted to force. Leonis and his mostly Mexican and Indian crewmen often shot intruders and prospective settlers on his lands. In what is now Hidden Hills, gunfire echoed through the canyons for weeks as one determined band of squatters tried to break the Basque's stranglehold on the West Valley. When the smoke finally cleared, the leader of the settlers was dead, and the rest of them retreated from the ranch.

Heavy-handed tactics like these made Leonis one of the most hated men in Southern California. So it wasn't surprising when after his death in 1889 in a wagon accident, rumors about murder began to spread.

Nothing ever came of the talk, though, and his Indian wife Espiritu

The notorious Miguel Leonis and wife haunt their old ranch in Calabasas.

held onto the estate until her death in 1906. In her last years, she lost most of the ranch lands in litigation. Her son from a previous marriage then took over the house, and he in turn sold it to a couple named Agoure in 1922.

Soon came stories that the house was haunted. The Agoures, and the owners that followed them, would often hear heavy footsteps on the stairs and in the upstairs hallways and rooms. Strange noises and untraceable odors were detected all over the house.

The most dramatic event was in the 1930s, when a woman living at the house was "saved" by an unseen presence. One night she leaned on a second-floor porch railing, heard a creaking sound, and then felt "strong hands" grip her shoulders and pull her back from the railing. Next day, an inspection at the place where she had stood showed that the railing was rotted and could have broken if she leaned a little more.

In more recent times, a visitor saw a ghostly form in the hallway and heard it crying *"Chichita, chichita"* (a corruption of chiquita, "little girl" in Spanish). Mrs. Pedro Orsua, one of the caretakers at the time, heard the startled visitor's story, and believed that the ghostly being was her grandmother, Espiritu Leonis, who used to call her by that nickname when she was a child.

Senor Leonis made an appearance, too, back in 1971. A house docent was sitting on the front porch waiting for the day's flock of tourists, when she and two companions saw "the shadow of a very tall man" suddenly appear on the living room door. The silhouette faded as quickly as it had appeared, but the three had no doubt that it belonged to Miguel Leonis, maverick Old West rancher come back to haunt the caretakers of his now-vanished empire.

The Leonis Adobe is open to the public Wed.-Sun. 1-4; phone (818) 712-0734.

Devil's Gate Reservoir *(adj. to Oak Grove Park Road at Pasadena-La Canada city boundaries)* This dry, brush-filled flood channel is appropriately named. It's the scene of a truly diabolical, tragic mystery.

The grim story begins on August 5, 1956, just a few miles east of Devil's Gate. That day, Donald Lee Baker, a 13-year old Azusan, went for a bike ride with Brenda Howell, 11, from Fort Bragg who was visiting relatives next door. They headed for the San Gabriel Reservoir that Sunday morning, and were last seen alive there that evening.

When they failed to return on Sunday night, their frightened parents notified police, who called out an all-points search for the missing children. Azusa police, Los Angeles County sheriffs, and hundreds of volunteers combed the suburbs and foothills of the San Gabriel Valley, while Navy frogmen plumbed the 60-foot depths of the reservoir.

After months of searching, only the children's bicycles and Brenda's jacket were recovered. No other trace of them has ever been found.

The hills claimed another young victim under even stranger circumstances on March 23, 1957. Eight-year old Tommy Bowman was hiking on a trail above Devil's Gate with his family, when he ran a few yards ahead of the others, rounded a corner...and disappeared.

When Tommy's family searched the brush and repeatedly called his name to no avail, a 400-member search party was sent out, complete with helicopters, mounted patrols, bloodhounds and professional wilderness trackers. After scouring the entire area for a week, hacking through chaparral and delving crevices and holes just off the trail, the search was called off. Rumors of kidnappers and child molesters were thoroughly investigated, and rejected. Tommy's disappearance has never been explained or solved.

Yet another child followed Tommy, Brenda and Donald into oblivion just three years later. Six-year old Bruce Kremen was on a hike with his YMCA group not far from where Tommy Bowman vanished, when he began to tire and fall behind the others. Thinking the boy was winded by the exercise and the high altitude, the group leader told Bruce to return to the camp—in plain sight just 300 yards away—and rest. The adult leader then watched Bruce walk the length of the wide, marked trail. When the boy was just yards away from camp, the man rejoined the other children.

But something got Bruce Kremen in those last few steps between the trailhead and the camp. He never made it back, and was never seen again.

Again, a massive search party tore the region apart. Again, kidnapping and molestation were discounted by investigators. And again, the San Gabriels claimed a young victim, leaving no clues, no suspects, no remains—and no solution to the case.

The disappearance of the four children remains one of Southern California's eeriest mysteries. To this day, no trace of them has ever been uncovered. And police, rangers and others are still at a loss to explain how Tommy Bowman could vanish just steps ahead of his family, or what came between little Bruce Kremen and the YMCA camp on the trail at Devil's Gate.

Elizabeth Lake *(17 mi. W of Palmdale on Elizabeth Lake Road)* Today, this mile-long mountain lake is a favorite playground for fishermen and boaters from the nearby Antelope Valley.

But in the 19th century, the lake was hated and feared by Spaniards and Americans. Legend had it that the Devil himself had created the lake from fire and brimstone, and that one of his monstrous pets dwelt beneath its murky waters.

The first white man who tried to settle here, a Don Pedro Carrillo, gave up only three months after building a fine ranch on the lakeshore in the 1830s. One night, a huge fire of unknown origin consumed all the ranch buildings, and he fled the area, muttering about how the *"Laguna del Diablo"* was driving him to an early grave.

The area remained deserted until 1855, when American squatters moved in. Though initially attracted by the stream-fed, fertile land and its beautiful surroundings, they too gave up. California's tough pioneers almost never left good land without a fight, but these homesteaders abandoned the area quietly, saying, "The whole infernal region is haunted."

In their wake came another Spanish don, Chico Lopez. Lopez thought that there was something a little odd about the lake, so he built his house a few miles from the water, using the surrounding territory for his ranch.

Things went smoothly until one day when Don Lopez was entertaining a visitor, Don Guillermo. Lopez's range boss, Chico Vasquez, galloped up to the house on horseback, exclaiming that "all the demons of

A dragonlike monster terrorized Elizabeth Lake many years ago.

song and story" were surfacing on the lake, lashing its waters and roaring hideously.

The three men rode swiftly to the lake, arriving just as a thunderous roar exploded from the water. Seconds later, a nauseating stench filled the air. (It was said that the odor lingered on the lake's reed-choked west end for years afterwards.) Then, a huge monster with enormous batlike wings broke the water's surface. While beast flapped its wings several times and kicked the muddy lake bottom with its legs, the men turned their terrified horses and galloped back to the ranch house.

The next day, Don Lopez returned to the lake with his heavily armed ranch hands, but the monster was nowhere in sight. Afterwards, it was whispered that a dragonlike creature could sometimes be seen flying in the night sky over Rancho Lopez. Lopez eventually quit the valley and sold out at a loss, claiming that his horses and cattle were disappearing at an alarming rate. Ranch hands and others blamed the monster of Elizabeth Lake for his losses.

The Lopez ranch lands were now the property of El Basquo Grande, Miguel Leonis (see **LOS ANGELES COUNTY: Calabasas:** *The Leonis Adobe*). The fearless Basque allegedly once chased the griffin back to the lake after it raided his stock pens, only to see it submerge beneath the muddy waters.

Another local man of the period, Don Felipe Rivera, claimed that he had seen the beast. Don Rivera said the monster was about 44 feet long, and had two wings, six legs and a head like a bulldog. A wildly exaggerated newspaper story published in October 1886 said Don Rivera swore "on the honor of a *hidalgo*" that he'd shot the beast six times with a Colt .44, and the bullets just bounced off, flattening like coins.

The creature was last seen flying east, and afterwards no longer haunted Elizabeth Lake. The *Tombstone (Ariz.) Epitaph* then printed a tall story in early 1890 about a 150-foot-long flying monster killed by two ranchers in the Huachuca Mountains west of Tombstone. Needless to say, the giant carcass was never recovered.

The Elizabeth Lake monster sounds like an elaborate, decades-long hoax, but some questions about the story have never been answered. Why did hardy American squatters flee the peaceful, fertile lake valley? And why did the honor-bound, prideful Spanish dons insist that a huge monster was living in the lake and stealing their cattle? What would these men gain by inviting public ridicule with such stories?

Perhaps the monster was "real," in a strange paraphysical sense. Many parapsychologists and anomalists have blamed psychic phenomena, hauntings and "monsters" like the Elizabeth Lake dragon on unknown geophysical causes. If earthquake faults and piezoelectric effects can light the night sky during quakes (see Part II, **SAN BENITO COUNTY: Hollister**), then, they say, perhaps the same forces can create fantastic mirages and illusions like flying monsters.

In fact, Elizabeth Lake sits directly over the San Andreas Fault. It's possible that the monster was a strange illusion, a chimera created by the same forces that occasionally strike California with more destructive fury than a dragon could ever muster. At any rate, the homeowners, boaters and fishermen at the lake are probably greatly relieved that they've never had to deal with the beast, phantom or not.

Though much of the lakefront is privately owned, Elizabeth Lake is accessible to the public on its west end; look for the turnoff to the National Forest recreation area just off the highway.

Hollywood: *The Hollywood Park Memorial Cemetery (6000 Santa Monica Blvd.)* Legends lie buried at this huge, parklike expanse of headstones and mausoleums...screen stars from old Hollywood, actors and actresses from the silent films and the Thirties classics.

Charlie Chaplin is entombed here. So is Rudolph Valentino, whose resting place is marked by a statue of him as "The Sheik." Tyrone Power, Douglas Fairbanks, Barbara LaMarr, Marion Davies, Cecil B. DeMille and other greats of Twenties and Thirties Hollywood lie here as well, along with more recent stars like Jayne Mansfield and Peter Finch.

One departed star here continues to act, undeterred by death and second-magnitude status in the old-Hollywood galaxy. For years, strange night lights and sounds have been reported in the vicinity of the Abbey of the Psalms, a huge mausoleum on the west end of the cemetery. One of the mausoleum's foyers is haunted, too, by a glowing presence that walks its marble floors.

The presence is thought to be the ghost of actor Clifton Webb, most famous for his acid-tongued roles in *Laura* and the original *Mr. Belvedere* series. Webb, who died in 1966, is reputed to haunt his old house in the Hollywood Hills as well.

Considering the myth-filled, tragic short lives of some of Memorial Park's residents (e.g., Valentino and Mansfield), why Webb became the park ghost is unclear. Perhaps he is playing the sarcastic, annoying Mr. Belvedere role in death as well as in life, vexing the living with his eerie presence.

The park is open every day from 8-5, and free maps are available at the Administration Building at the gate.

Directions: To find Webb's crypt in the Abbey, go to the main entrance on West Avenue, and turn down the first hallway on the left. It's about two-thirds of the way down, on the left side.

Long Beach: *The Queen Mary (Pier J, end of Hwy 710)* The Other World has followed this luxury liner since her maiden voyage in 1934. Just after the big ship was launched, London astrologer Lady Mabel Fortescue-Harrison told newspapers, "The Queen Mary, launched today, will know her greatest fame and popularity when she never sails another mile and never carries another paying passenger."

The psychic noblewoman was right. Now permanently lodged at Pier J, the ship is one of Los Angeles' most famous tourist attractions, a 390-room floating hotel which also hosts tours, conventions and maritime exhibits. It's also home to a number of ghosts.

All sorts of spooky things have happened over the length of the 1,019-foot, 81,237-ton liner. Lights flicker and doors slam unaided by human hands on the "G" deck, thought to be the location of the ship's morgue.

Another hot spot is the swimming pool, where the ghost of a middle-aged woman in an archaic swimsuit sometimes dives into the empty basin. She's thought to have drowned there. Some people have seen a young, mini-skirted woman pace around the pool area and disappear behind a pillar. Sounds of shouting and splashing have been heard at the deserted poolside deck as well.

More unnerving phenomena have been reported in one of the kitchens. During World War II, when the ship was used as a troop transport, a brawl erupted in the galley, and a cook was shoved into an oven and burned to death. Now, near the site of his death, light switches turn themselves on and off, dishes move under their own power and utensils mysteriously vanish.

Other shipboard phantoms include an elegantly dressed "woman in white" who hangs around the salon's piano, a ghostly officer who walks near the bridge, and a black-bearded man in coveralls who rides the engine-room escalator.

For some reason, the engine-room area is the most haunted place on the ship. Staff members and tour guides who go there report clanging and knocking sounds, chains being whipped and dangled by unseen hands, and balls of light moving slowly across the walls.

Tom Hennessy, a *Long Beach Press-Telegram* columnist who was initially skeptical about ghosts on the *Queen Mary*, spent a night near the ship's engine room and came out a believer. During his stay, he was menaced by moving oil drums, felt the vibrations of some invisible presence walking towards him on a catwalk, and heard clanging noises that stopped when he approached them.

Hennessy's eeriest experience came at 3:33 AM, when he heard two or three men talking in the deserted propeller-shaft room. He distinctly made out the words, "...turning the lights off," from one of them. A security guard later told him that no live people had been near the shaft room when he heard the conversation, and that other people had heard disembodied voices there as well.

At present, the *Queen Mary* is virgin territory for researchers, psychic investigators and ghost hunters. Few of the ship's resident spooks have been identified, and the incidents that bind them to the immobile ship are mostly lost to history.

The Queen Mary is open to the public from 9-9 in summer, and from 10-6 the rest of the year; phone (213) 435-3511.

Los Angeles Though most of its haunted houses are privately owned or otherwise inaccessible, the City of the Angels isn't without its mysterious places. Here are four of them:

Builders of the Adytum Temple (5105 N. Figueroa) A nondescript little brick building in the Highland Park district houses what might be the most unusual church in Los Angeles.

The organization, known as Builders of the Adytum, was founded in 1920 by Paul Foster Case. Case was a precocious expert in both the use and symbolism of Tarot cards, and in Kabbalism, the ancient, complex system of Jewish mysticism. At the tender age of 26, he assumed leadership of the powerful Order of the Golden Dawn, a seminal occult society whose members included W.B. Yeats, Arthur Machen and Aleister Crowley. Case became embroiled in scandal, though, and resigned his post to found his own Kabbalistic mystery school, Builders of the Adytum, in New York City.

Case moved B.O.T.A. to Los Angeles in 1933. Here, it thrived under the ministry of Ann Davies, who was Case's star pupil and took over after he died in 1954. Davies was an intelligent, charismatic woman who added much to Case's doctrines and drew many people to B.O.T.A. through her services and correspondence courses.

Today, B.O.T.A. is as active as ever, and its temple is open to the public for Sunday services. The temple walls are decorated with large, bright paintings of the Tarot cards and with banners emblazoned with Hebrew lettering. The black and white Pillars of Solomon flank the altar's centerpiece, a full-color diagram of the Kabbalistic Tree. Services feature organ recitals, singing, incense-burning, angelic name-chanting, hand-raising prayers, and sermons on Tarot, Kabbalism and the other Mysteries. The highlight of the ritual is the silent meditation, when the lights dim and the illuminated Kabbalistic Tree glows in the incense-hazed darkness.

B.O.T.A. also offers in-depth classes in Tarot, Kabbalism and Hermetic mysteries. Dues-paying members can study either by mail or at the temple's Thursday night classes. Unlike the usually Eastern-oriented New Age sects and gurus, B.O.T.A.'s studies are based in a solidly Judeo-Christian and Western system of thought.

Like San Jose's Rosicrucians (q.v.), Builders of the Adytum preserves and propagates the Western mystical tradition in the modern world. A visit to its unorthodox temple is a must for anyone interested in this highly influential spiritual heritage.

B.O.T.A. holds its public services on Sunday at 11 AM; phone (213) 255-7141.

Downtown Deep beneath the heart of Los Angeles' financial district, hundreds of feet below the huge downtown edifices that house banks, corporate offices and government agencies, lies another city remembered only in obscure Indian legends, an underground world built by a strange race that vanished five thousand years ago.

At least that's what mining engineer W. Warren Shufelt claimed in the January 29, 1934 *Los Angeles Times*. According to reporter Jean Bosquet, Shufelt was ready to dig up downtown L.A. in search of this ancient subterranean civilization.

Shufelt had first heard of the city in a Hopi legend about "the Lizard People." They were a fabled lost race who had built 13 great underground cities on the Pacific Coast after a huge holocaust swept the Southwest back around 3000 BC. The subterranean settlements were constructed to shelter the tribe against future disasters, and housed a thousand families each, along with stockpiles of food. As the story has it, they bored out the tunnels of their subsurface homes with a "chemical solution" that melted solid bedrock. Among other things, the Lizard People possessed troves of golden tablets that chronicled their race's history, the origin of humankind, and the story of the world back to creation.

A Hopi chief told Shufelt that the vanished race's capital city was located under present-day downtown Los Angeles. After surveying the area, Shufelt showed up on the Banning property at North Hill street and sank a 350-foot shaft straight down, digging for what he said was a "treasure room" directly underneath. Shufelt said he had located gold in the catacombs below with the aid of his "radio X-ray."

This peculiar instrument, which was sort of a glorified dowsing pendulum, had also helped Shufelt map the location and extent of the underground tunnels. He said that the subterranean city was shaped like a giant lizard, with the tail tapering out beneath the Central Library, and the head in the vicinity of Chavez Ravine (now Dodger Stadium). The "key room," the chamber that contained the map of the city and the directory to the gold tablets, lay several hundred feet under the present site of Times-Mirror Square. Shufelt also claimed that he'd traced passages stretching to the region around the Southwest Museum, and said that ventilation tunnels extended westward, opening at the Pacific Ocean.

Despite all of his extensive mapping and plotting of the treasure-filled underground city, Shufelt never actually found it. The newspaper accounts were never followed up, Shufelt disappeared, and the whole mysterious, improbable business was written off as a hoax. Since then, inexplicable tunnels have been unearthed in downtown Los Angeles, but they've usually been explained away as the work of smugglers hiding illegal Chinese laborers in the last century.

But Shufelt wasn't the only modern Californian who believed that an ancient underground city lay beneath Los Angeles.As a postscript to this strange little tale, let's look at the vision of Miss Edith Elden Robinson of Pico Rivera, California, which appeared in the highly respected American Society for Psychical Research's journal.

On the evening of December 22, 1933, five weeks before Shufelt's excavations hit the pages of the Times, the clairvoyant Miss Robinson envisioned "a vast city...in mammoth tunnels extending to the sea-shore." She said that the tunnels had been constructed by a vanished race to protect themselves from danger, and to provide access to the sea.

Who knows? Maybe this fabulous subterranean city really existed. Perhaps it's even filled with latter-day Lizard People who live hidden and unsuspected hundreds of feet below modern Los Angeles, emerging only furtively to watch the 20th-century barbarians slowly strangle their own surface-level civilization with smog, traffic and urban sprawl. (The Lizard People are said to have been another one of Mount Shasta's resident lost races; see its entry in **Part I**.)

Griffith Park The "Curse of Griffith Park" is one of Old Los Angeles' most persistent legends. Though many historians deny that landowner Antonio Coronel's spread had ever been hexed, a curious series of disasters and tragedies did befall him and others who owned the 3,000-acre tract.

The legend begins on the day that Don Antonio Feliz died of smallpox in 1863. Don Feliz, a wealthy landowner whose holdings included what is now Griffith Park, left most of his holdings to his friend Don Antonio Coronel. The rest was divided up between relatives.

But Don Feliz's blind, 17-year-old niece, Dona Petranilla, was given nothing. Enraged at losing her childhood home and family wealth to Don Antonio, she confronted the man who had received what she knew was her rightful inheritance.

In *On the Old West Coast*, local historian Horace Bell says she screamed a venomous hex at Don Antonio: "This is what I hurl upon your head: Your falsity shall be your ruin! The substance of the Feliz family shall be your curse! The lawyer that assisted you in your infamy, and the judge, shall fall beneath the same curse! The one shall die an untimely death, the other in blood and violence! You, senor, shall know misery in your age and though you die rich your substance shall go to vile persons!...Misfortune, crime and death shall follow those who covet these remains!" Dona Petranilla also cursed Don Antonio's lands and cattle with blight and barrenness, called down a torrent to wash away his land, and then dropped dead at his feet.

Modern historians, however, dismiss this story as a fable, and say that the often-unreliable Bell composed the curse. They point out that Dona Petranilla hadn't been completely cheated; her aunt, Maria Ignacio Verdugo, would continue to provide the blind girl with a lifelong home.

Be that as it may, a mysterious series of disasters did strike Griffith Park's various owners and the land itself. True to the curse, Don Antonio did grow old and rich from inheritances and deeds, but at the cost of personal tragedy as relatives died around him.

When Coronel himself passed on at 80, his young American widow inherited his estate. After remarrying, she and her new husband began to fight over the Coronel wealth. A messy divorce case ensued, and the sharklike lawyers that swarmed around the couple consumed most of the inheritance, perhaps fulfilling the Dona's prediction that "vile persons" would devour Coronel's fortune.

Don Antonio's own lawyer, who held administration rights to the ranch, was later killed in a drunken brawl. The judge who probated Antonio Feliz's will was said to have met an untimely end as well.

Griffith Park was next owned by Leon Baldwin. The wealthy Baldwin tried to run a ranch and dairy on the land, but a terrible streak of luck ruined him. So bad was his fortune that he ended up losing the property to mortgages. Baldwin himself was later murdered by Mexican bandits.

The land's next, and final, private owner was "Colonel" Griffith J. Griffith, a Welsh-born financier. Famous for his aristocratic pretensions and his uncanny knack for locating gold and silver deposits, Griffith too, felt Dona Petranilla's curse. A violent storm in March 1884 washed away much of the land and its foliage, and ranch hands swore that during the deluge they saw the ghost of old Antonio Feliz cursing and threatening all who dwelt on his rancho.

In 1896, Colonel Griffith shocked Los Angeles by turning the entire 3,000-acre property over to the City for use as a public park. But this monumental act of generosity, which has perpetuated Griffith's name, didn't quite save him from the ranch's jinx. Seven years later, a demented, paranoid Griffith tried to kill his wife in a Santa Monica hotel room. Pleading temporary insanity, he served a two-year stretch at San Quentin, and emerged with his reputation permanently damaged.

In modern times, Griffith Park has become America's largest urban park. Millions of Angelenos have enjoyed it without incident, though some are still quick to blame the curse when death or disaster strikes the land. If Dona Petranilla's hex was indeed responsible for the tragedies that followed Griffith Park's wealthy owners, it seems to have lifted now that the common people play in the hills, meadows and groves.

337 S. Main St. It's now just a disused, fenced-off parking lot on Skid Row facing an uncertain future. But around the turn of the century, this address boasted Los Angeles' most famous theater—the Belasco. When vaudeville was in its prime, the theater hosted performers who would make their marks on early Hollywood years later. W.C. Fields and Lewis Stone were just two of the greats who performed here.

But as Main Street declined, so did the Belasco. By the mid-Sixties, it had become the Follies, and featured striptease instead of theater. It had also picked up a ghost.

Around 1965, strippers, stagehands and night watchmen at the Follies began to tell eerie stories of a pretty, red-haired young woman who wandered the backstage area. She was always clad in a white negligee, they said, and often appeared on the circular staircase, fading into nothingness when approached.

The redheaded ghost was also blamed for other strange phenomena at the Follies. Once, the manager's wife and a caretaker were chatting in a dressing room when an empty clay vase exploded just inches away from them. Ropes holding stage backdrops often vibrated and swayed by themselves, and stagehands swore that the ropes would stop moving only when they were asked to!

Follies employees said that the ghost was a stripper who had once trod the club's runway. Deeply depressed, the woman had hanged herself in the basement, but had returned to haunt the Follies. Apparently, tragedies were not uncommon around the club—a scene painter who worked and lived there papered the walls of his little room with lurid newspaper accounts of Follies girls who were murder victims, suicides or otherwise died untimely deaths.

As the years went by, Main Street degenerated into a slum, and the old Follies building was demolished. The redheaded ghost hasn't been reported since; it's probable that the only spirits you'll see today at 337 S. Main are in the cheap wine bottles discarded by the neighborhood's down-and-out inhabitants.

Palos Verdes Peninsula All Bob Meistrell wanted was a few lobsters.

But he found something much more unusual and valuable on the sandy sea bottom here on a December day in 1975, 35 feet below the choppy currents off Palos Verdes Peninsula. When the crustaceans eluded him, Meistrell started digging for abalones, and instead uncovered a doughnut-shaped, 280-pound stone that looked man-made and ancient. Intrigued by the strange rock, he and diving partner Wayne Baldwin hauled it to the surface, and brought it to Meistrell's surf shop in Redondo Beach.

News of their find reached marine archeologists Larry Pierson and James Moriarty III at the University of San Diego. Pierson and Moriarty visited the site, and divers there soon brought more curious sandstone objects from the ocean floor. The two academics then spent several years having the finds analyzed at geological labs, and corresponding with scientists in Japan, Taiwan and China.

Their amazing conclusion: The stones were anchors and ballasts from a Chinese ship that had visited North America 1500 years before Columbus. Though some suggested that the ship had been torn from anchorage in Korea by a storm and blown across the Pacific, subsequent underwater excavations revealed two trailing anchors lying in deeper water directly behind the wreck. Pierson believed that the crew had thrown them overboard in a last-ditch attempt to save the ship from wrecking on Palos Verdes' notorious offshore reefs. The stone anchors were the only wreck remains that the intervening tides and centuries hadn't rotted away, and they were found to be made of sandstone native to south China.

Orientalists and others had long suspected that the ancient Chinese were the true "discoverers" of America. Scholar Henriette Mertz, in her book *Pale Ink*, carefully examined the legendary Chinese account of the land of Fu-Sang, a continent-sized land mass many thousands of miles east of China. Translating Chinese distance measurements into miles, she found that the stories placed Fu-Sang exactly at the California coast. She retraced the adventurers' movements across the fabled land, and found that their descriptions of the sights matched such landmarks as Mount Shasta, the La Brea Tar Pits and the Grand Canyon. Ms. Mertz believed that two different expeditions, centuries apart, had reached Fu-Sang and ventured as far east as Texas. She even suggested that a bearded Chinese Buddhist monk who ministered to the Mexican Indians was deified by them, and entered Aztec mythology as the great god Quetzalcoatl!

Farfetched as Ms. Mertz' claims might seem, the ancient Chinese did have the sea power necessary to cross the Pacific. Centuries before the Europeans, Chinese navigators possessed such naval technology as balanced rudders, watertight compartments and compasses.

In addition, Meistrell's anchor wasn't the first erratic ancient Chinese artifact to show up in North America. A year before Meistrell uncovered the stone anchor, a U.S. Geological Survey dredging operation 75 miles off the California shore had pulled up a similar stone relic. And earlier in the century, inexplicable Chinese inscriptions and relics had turned up around the West. Archaic Chinese rock writing had been found in a Nevada canyon, and a peculiar little idol covered with ancient Chinese characters was unearthed in Granby, Colorado...two more pieces in a vast, centuries-old Chinese puzzle.

The discovery may be the best challenge yet to orthodox American historians who deny that the continent was "discovered" before 1000 AD. For years, they had denied that ancient Europeans and Africans had visited America, despite the Phoenician urns, Celtic stone cairns and Roman coins that kept turning up on the New England coast. Now, from America's western shore, came a new affront to "accepted" history: some doughnut-shaped rocks tossed into the ocean 2,000 years ago, by Chinese sailors wrecked on the coast of wave-lashed Palos Verdes.

ORANGE COUNTY

Buena Park: *Coyote Creek flood channel (N of Franklin between King-man & Fullerton)* On the night of May 10, 1982, Bigfoot made his first appearance in Southern California suburbia, 40 miles south of his stronghold in the northern San Gabriel Mountains (see **LOS ANGELES COUNTY: Big Rock Canyon**).

The beast showed up in the flood channel behind the Executive Park Apartments on 7601 Franklin St. Residents there swore that an eight- or nine-foot tall, hairy, smelly, two-legged creature walked behind the building that night, roaring and growling like a beast from hell.

Among the witnesses were three teenaged boys: Bennie Hinsley, and brothers Chris and Raymond Bennett. At about 9:30 PM, they saw the beast stumbling around in the flood channel. Chirping crickets and croaking frogs were suddenly silent as the beast floundered in the mud and water. The three boys watched it for almost an hour, until it loped away, heading west.

Humans then invaded the channel over the next two days. Investigators made plaster casts of big footprints found in the channel, and over 100 locals lined its concrete walls, hoping for a glimpse of the suburban Sasquatch. They were disappointed, though, as the monster failed to make a second showing.

Local police, who had been irritated by the reports and skeptical from the start, finally "solved" the mystery. "Buenafoot," they said, was nothing more than a hairy, smelly, ill-mannered local transient well known to them. They pointed out that the bearded, long-haired hobo stood 6'3", and could easily have been mistaken in the dark for a hirsute monster.

But the many witnesses on Franklin Street stuck to their stories. They swore that the creature they had seen was at least eight feet tall, and had sounded like a cross "between Godzilla and a gorilla." They also doubted that most vagrants had size 16 feet.

Coyote Creek may be a harbinger of things to come. As Los Angeles' urban sprawl intrudes on the ranges of such zoologically-accepted creatures as the coyote and the mountain lion, these wild animals have shown up in the "urban" settings, now hunting pets instead of small game. Perhaps as the Sasquatches' territories disappear under asphalt and concrete, they will be more commonly seen in residential neighborhoods than in their traditional backwoods haunts.

Costa Mesa: *Santa Ana River Jetty* Surfers fled the waves after they saw a "long black eel" swimming just 60 feet offshore here on November 2, 1983. Witness Young Hutchinson told a *Costa Mesa Daily Pilot reporter* that the beast "was really moving, like a whale with a purpose....We got the hell out of there and paddled for shore." Hutchinson also said that the big creature wasn't a whale, since he had seen many whales in the local waters before, and this animal was serpentlike, lacking a cetacean's dorsal fins and distinctive motions. He had initially been reluctant to report the sighting, he said, but was encouraged when he read about similar beasts seen up north (see **MARIN COUNTY: Stinson Beach**).

But it wasn't the first time strange creatures had visited the waters off the Orange Coast. Back in the early part of the century, Southern California's sport-fishing fraternity was all abuzz with stories of a giant sea monster sighted in these waters.

In his book *Tight Lines*, big-game fisherman and Tuna Club secretary Ralph Bandini remembered the day in 1919 he first laid eyes on the huge beast. Though he had heard many stories about the creature, he had never seen it until one day when he was fishing for tuna in the San Clemente Channel. Bandini was about ten miles south of Catalina, when one of his crewman, Percy Neal, shouted for him to look aft. Bandini then saw something huge, dark and shining rise high out of the water about a mile away.

Almost a year later, Bandini got an even better look at the leviathan. He was fishing for marlin in the Channel with fellow sportsman Smith Warren, when the two men saw a dark, massive beast break the surface about 400 yards away. The creature lifted its six-foot thick neck and head about 10 feet above the water, and its dull, dinner-plate-sized eyes gazed straight at their boat. Bandini said that the monster seemed to have a mane of coarse hair. He also noticed that the swelling waves didn't rise the creature as they would a whale, which meant the serpent must have been enormous.

Bandini saw the creature on two other occasions, though not at such close range. Many other Tuna Club members also reported the beast in the same waters throughout the Twenties and Thirties.

Years later, the San Clemente Monster resurfaced in the presence of Sam Randazzo, a commercial fisherman. On June 8, 1953, a "Thing" with a 10-foot-long, six-foot wide neck and huge eyes appeared right next to Randazzo's boat. Randazzo and crew immediately reported the incident to the Coast Guard. A few other fishermen also saw unidentified giant sea creatures in the area during the Fifties, but then nothing was reported for years. The Orange County sea serpents appeared to have moved on.

But if Young Hutchinson can be believed, the leviathans are making a comeback. And this time, they aren't harassing deep-sea fishermen out on the open sea, but are terrifying surfers just yards away from Orange County's exclusive beachfront neighborhoods.

O'Neill Regional Park: *Trabuco Creek* This tree-lined *arroyo* is home to *La Llorona*, one of the most feared phantoms in all of Mexican legend and lore.

La Llorona("the crier") gets her name from her ghostly, bansheelike wail. Legend has it that she was an evil woman who cheated on her husband, and drowned her three children because they kept her from her lover. God then condemned her to walk the earth for all eternity, searching for her drowned children.

It's said that she steals the souls of living children, and she's often invoked by Mexican mothers to frighten naughty *ninos*. Tradition also has it that if you see her, you or someone close to you will die. The origin of the legend is unknown, though some folklorists believe it may go back to Aztec times.

Many modern Mexican-Americans believe in *La Llorona*and swear that she still bedevils the living. They say she still walks Southern California's hill country at night, her long, jet-black hair and black dress blowing in the wind, an evil counterpart to California's many "Women in White" ghosts. But where her face should be, there's only a blank, white space.

*La Llorona*has been reported all over Southern California, usually in heavily Hispanic neighborhoods, but most often around Trabuco Creek. The creek is rumored to be the spot where the wicked woman drowned her children in the distant past. And on moonlit nights you can see her black-clad, faceless form bending over at the creekbed, her pale arms elbow-deep in the waters, searching for her drowned children.

San Juan Capistrano This town is home to at least five ghosts, in two locations:

Los Rios Street Another "Woman in White" is this avenue's resident phantom. Black-haired, clad in a white gown and often accompanied by a black dog, she appears out of a white fog to vex and harass the living.

She's the ghost of a young woman who fell in love with a man living here in the 19th century. When he spurned her attentions, she poisoned herself on his front porch. For almost 90 years, locals say, her tragic shade has haunted Los Rios Street.

One of her prime haunts is the big pepper tree in front of the Rios Adobe (itself reportedly haunted by a male ghost). Years ago, a young man passed by this tree late at night, and ran home in a terror, gasping that the Woman in White and her black dog were following him.

The Woman in White was still bothering Los Rios residents as recently as the late 1970s. A stewardess living on the street then was tormented by an invisible force that moved objects around her house and knocked all the ornaments off her Christmas tree. She thought that it was just a common poltergeist, and waited for it to pass (as these destructive phenomena usually do), when one night a white fog filled her house, and the white-clad spirit revealed herself as the culprit.

Desperate to rid the house of the annoying ghost, the stewardess held a seance. According to the story, the spirit appeared and agreed to leave the premises. But Los Rios residents say she's been back a few times since then, still bound to earth by her tragic death and her penchant for mischief.

Mission San Juan Capistrano Just south of Los Rios Street lies this mission, famous worldwide for the swallows that return here every spring. It's also famous among ghost hunters as one of California's most haunted missions.

The mission's best-known ghost is Magdalena, the spirit of a young woman killed in a tragic accident back in the missionary days. Caught in an illicit love affair, she was ordered to do penitence by carrying a candle around the mission grounds for one day: December 8, 1812. When the great earthquake of that date hit, Magdalena was inside the Great Stone Church, dutifully carrying her candle. The walls of the church collapsed, killing her, and it's said that if one gazes at a certain window of the wrecked church, sometimes the face of a sad young woman will stare out, lit softly by a single candle.

San Juan Capistrano also boasts a sinister, ghostly monk. The phantom friar, clad in a hooded robe, silently paces the inner courtyard. Don't get too close to him, though; legend has it that if you gaze into his hood, the sight of his face will turn your hair gray and stop your heart.

There's also a "headless soldier" who patrols the grounds, and the inevitable invisible bellringers who've invaded the tower on several occasions.

In addition to all this, the mission's graveyard was the site of a semi-famous experiment by Fullerton's Psychic Science Investigators. PSI

Mission San Juan Capistrano's Great Stone Church, haunt of Magdelena.

members wanted to determine whether disembodied voices could be taped at such places, so they left a tape recorder overnight in the cemetery, posting guards nearby to make sure nobody tampered with it. In the morning, they played the tape back, and two unexplained voices spoke.

One whispered in a breathy voice, "I have to give you my name." The other ghostly voice said, quite plainly, "I'm scared." The voices have never been traced or explained.

The Mission is open daily from 7:30-5; phone (714) 493-1424.

RIVERSIDE COUNTY

Blythe: *The Blythe Intaglios (17 mi N of Blythe on Hwy 95 at the "Giant Desert Figures" historic landmark)* Not too far from the Colorado River, on the low hills just west of Highway 95, lies one of the most spectacular ancient creations in California.

Unseen by whites until the 20th century, these huge figures hidden on a flat desert floor were discovered from the air. In 1930, aviator George Palmer was flying over the area when he spotted outlines of a man, a woman, a horse, a coiled snake and "horseshoes" on the top of a mesa. He reported his find to the Southwest Museum, but lacking funds because of the Depression, they couldn't investigate the figures until 1952.

The Intaglios were seen again by Army fliers on desert maneuvers in the Forties. This time, the National Geographic Society and the Smithsonian Institution sent airborne archeologists to the site. An extensive article appeared in the *National Geographic* of September 1952, with aerial photos that showed the huge figures to the world.

Primitive artists created the figures using the intaglio process. They scraped away a shallow layer of dark surface soil and rock to reveal light-colored soil underneath, and piled dark gravel around the figures to outline them. Though portions of the effigies can be seen if one is standing right next to them, they are virtually invisible just a few feet away, and there are no nearby hills affording clear views of them.

The larger of the human figures, thought to be the outline of a woman, is about 175 feet long. Her outflung arms span 158 feet. Her male companion is about 95 feet tall. There's also a 53-foot-long, four-footed creature that's been alternatively identified as a panther, a coyote or a horse. The latter interpretation is especially popular among revisionist anthropologists who insist that horses lived on the North American continent long before the Spanish brought their mounts here.

The coiled-snake figure has been mostly obliterated. Off-road vehicle drivers ground it into dust, and nearly destroyed the other figures as well. "Desecration" is probably a better word for these actions, considering that the effigies were probably religious symbols.

Today, the Intaglios are protected by two lines of fences, and are open to the public at all times as a State Historic Monument. Their creators are long dead and their exact purpose remains a mystery, but the desert figures have finally been granted protection and well-deserved recognition as the most colossal of California's many cryptic Indian drawings.

Joshua Tree National Monument Mystery hangs over this vast expanse of rock piles, stark mountain ranges and the twisted yucca trees that give the park its name.

Perhaps because of its desolately beautiful, otherworldly landscape, the Joshua Tree region has long attracted eccentrics living on the farthest edges of Southern Californian exurbia. UFO devotees have often insisted that there is a secret spaceship base hidden somewhere in the brush-dotted hills. They say that the strange lights commonly seen in the desert night sky are extraterrestrial craft visiting the base. UFO cult-leader George Adamski claimed that he got a saucer ride from "long-haired Venusians" aboard one of the ships cruising above Highway 177, just east of the park.

Other desert residents tell of bizarre happenings in and around the

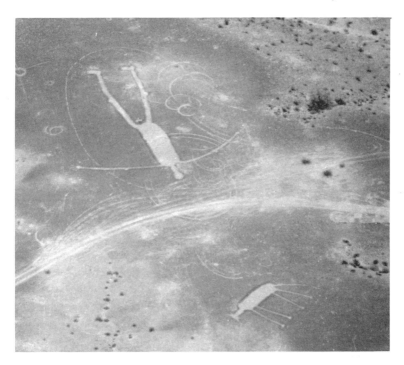

The Blythe Intaglios, from the air (above), and from the ground.

park. They've seen camper trucks dematerialize on the Morongo Valley highway, furtive three-fingered aliens buy supplies in Joshua Tree drugstores, and glowing, robotlike humanoids wander across the National Monument outback.

One of the oddest places in Joshua Tree National Monument is the Gram Parsons "memorial" on the north side of Cap Rock, in the center of the park. Parsons, a talented musician who almost singlehandedly invented the country-rock genre, died at the Joshua Tree Inn on September 19, 1973 of what was rumored to be a massive drug overdose.

When his body was at Los Angeles International Airport, en route to the family burial plot back in Georgia, his friend Phil Kaufman snatched Parsons' coffin off the freight ramp. Kaufman, who had once produced Charles Manson's solo album, then loaded the coffin into an improvised hearse and drove out to Cap Rock, one of Parson's favorite hangouts in the park. There he and an accomplice laid the corpse out on the desert floor, and set it aflame in a macabre little cremation ceremony. The two men were arrested soon afterwards, but were released when it was found that no California laws prohibited body-snatching or impromptu cremations.

After his death, Parsons became something of a minor youth cult figure, and the little grotto at Cap Rock where the strange ceremony took place is covered with little eulogies, quotes from Parsons' songs and fanciful drawings left by fans. Sometimes offerings are scattered there as well. It's a modest monument, but a fitting one to this strange land's most famous devotee and victim.

Lake Elsinore Since 1884, lakeside residents here have occasionally seen a large, unidentified creature swimming in the lake.

The beast was seen most recently in 1970. Lakefront resident Bonnie Pray, who spotted the monster twice that winter, said it was about 12 feet long, three feet wide, and jet-black in color. The creature was shaped like a giant snake and swam with an "undulating motion."

Shortly after Ms. Pray's sighting, three Lake Elsinore State Recreation Area officials sighted something huge swimming in the lake. But they couldn't quite agree on what they had seen. One official described it as a black, shiny "thing" that rose slowly out of the water. Another said that the beast had a head, ears and a long tail that splashed the water. And the third witness dismissed it as a giant catfish.

Local Indians may have known of the creature as well. A legend describes how the lake was created when an evil "sea serpent" god was being chased by his rival through the mountains. The serpent's tail sideswiped a mountain lake, and water spilled into the valley, forming Lake Elsinore. Why inland Indians associated the lake with a sea serpent is a mystery; perhaps they had other, now-forgotten traditions about the lake monster.

Another mystery is the fact that Lake Elsinore dried up completely twice in this century. Since no 12-foot black serpents were reported flopping around in the muddy, exposed bottom, skeptics say the beast is a myth. In response, believers say that the serpent could have holed up while the lake was dry.

Lake Elsinore is accessible to the public at the State Recreation Area on its northwest shore, as well as at two public parks in the town of Lake Elsinore, Elm Grove Park and Ramada Park.

Maze Rock County Park A big, striking petroglyph of unknown origin graces this tiny mountain park.

The Maya's distant ancestors may have created Maze Rock.

Inscribed on a large boulder, the three-foot-square figure is a maze formed by four interlocking swastikas. The design is almost unknown among Indian petroglyphs, and archeologists attribute it to the so-called "Maze Culture," who left only one similar design, miles to the south in San Diego County. Maze Rock has also been explained as everything from a 15,000 year-old remnant of the "Cascadians," the alleged ancestors of the Maya, to a religious symbol left by Chinese Buddhist monks at about 500 AD. The latter theory is especially favored by historians seeking to prove that the Chinese beat Columbus to North America by at least 1000 years (see **LOS ANGELES COUNTY: Palos Verdes Peninsula**).

Directions: From Hemet, drive 4.8 miles west on Highway 74, turn right on California Avenue, and follow it to the park. Maze Rock Park is open to the public every day, all day; phone (714) 787-2553.

SAN BERNARDINO COUNTY

Calico Early Man Site This extremely controversial archeological dig, high in the Calico Mountains, is either the biggest and most successful scientific hoax since the Piltdown Man, or a bombshell that will destroy many traditional theories and views of the prehistoric New World.

The site was discovered back in 1958, when archeologists surveying an Ice Age-era lake called the Manix Basin found what looked like Old Stone Age artifacts on the basin's surface.

The artifacts soon touched off a heated debate among experts. Many archeologists insisted that the rock objects were nothing more than "geofacts," false artifacts created by nature. Others were deeply impressed by the finds.

Among the latter group was Ruth DeEtte Simpson, who took some of the artifacts to Dr. Louis S.B. Leakey in London. Dr. Leakey, who was famous for his excavation of Olduvai Gorge in Africa, visited the site in May 1963, and eventually obtained funds from the National Geographic Society for a full-scale excavation that began in November 1964. Leakey served as the site's Project Director until his death in 1972.

Since 1964, three master pits have been excavated, and over 12,000 stone items have been found. Most common are objects that appear to be hand-held scrapers, choppers, axes, gravers, perforators and sawing tools, many of which show use-wear. Some of the tools resemble similar items found in China, Korea and Siberia.

The real shocker came when the tools were given uranium-thorium dating tests. Analyzed at both the U.S. Geological Survey lab and the University of Southern California, the artifacts turned out to be 200,000 years old, give or take about 20,000 years. Since official estimates placed humans in the New World no earlier than about 10,000 BC, one can understand why the crude rock tools ignited a firestorm of controversy.

Because of the tools' extreme age, pro-Calico theorists believe that they could not possibly have been made by Indians or paleo-Indians. They would have been the work of a more primitive human subspecies, possibly Neanderthals or even Homo erectus. Orthodox archeologists deny that either of these proto-human groups ever occupied the Western Hemisphere.

But if they had been here, current views of late human evolution would have to be revised. New World archeology would also take on a whole new meaning and importance. Because of these potentially devastating changes, it's easy to see why many mainline scholars refuse to accept the Calico artifacts.

Calico's partisans have opened the site to the public. There are displays of the controversial artifacts, and guided tours take visitors to the excavation site. A visit is highly recommended; this is a rare chance to see what may turn out to be the most important prehistoric dig in the Western Hemisphere.

Directions: From Barstow, take Highway 15 north to the Mineola Road exit, and turn left. Follow the signs to the "Calico Early Man Site" and be prepared for about 1.5 miles of rough, unpaved road.

The site is open Wed.-Sun. from 8:30-4:30. Phone (619) 256-3591.

Giant Rock Airport The 40-foot tall, white-domed "Integratron" is the showpiece of this UFO cult's fenced-in compound.

The Integratron was built by the late George van Tassel, one of the original postwar UFO contactees. Like George Adamski and George Hunt Williamson, Van Tassel claimed he was taken for a ride on a spaceship by benevolent aliens (who seemed to have a weakness for humans named George). He also said that these beings often contacted him afterwards through both "energy beams" and personal visits.

Van Tassel soon turned his experiences into a religion. Feeling that the Giant Rock area was a "natural cone of receptivity" for UFOs, he organized a church here, known as the "Ministry of Universal Wisdom," to communicate with alien visitors. From 1954 on, the Ministry held UFO contactee conventions at Giant Rock, and devotees of the Space Brothers came from all over the country to have tent revival-style gatherings and

The mysterious "Integratron" rises ominously over Giant Rock Airport.

receive wisdom from the all-knowing aliens. Sometimes mysterious lights hovered in the night sky above the meetings.

The Space Brothers are said to have given Van Tassel the idea for the Integratron as well. The domed device is allegedly used to rejuvenate aging cells and reverse gravity, and can even allow one to travel in time. Naturally, this top-secret, dangerous device is heavily guarded and fenced off, and it's become something of a local landmark.

When Van Tassel died in 1978, there was a dispute over the Integratron's future uses. A man bought the building and announced plans to turn it into a disco. Horrified, Van Tasselites around the country rallied and bought back the Integratron. Today it's again in the hands of UFO devotees.

Directions: From Yucca Valley, drive north on Highway 247 10.5 miles, and turn right at Reches Road. Drive 2.3 miles east, turn left at Belfield, and follow it to the end. The Integratron is at 2477 Belfield. The dome is on fenced-off, guarded private property; please restrict visits to views from the road.

Santa Ana River Bridge *(4.5 mi S of the San Bernardino Fwy., on Riverside Ave.)* Charles Wetzel never dreamed he'd become the hero of one of Southern California's most bizarre events.

Wetzel, a 24-year-old Riverside resident, was driving along Riverside

Avenue on the night of November 8, 1958. Suddenly, something jumped out of the bushes and blocked his car just north of the Santa Ana River bridge. The "something" was a creature from a nightmare. Standing in the glare of Wetzel's headlights, the thing was about six feet tall, with a "round, scarecrowish head like something out of Halloween." It had a protuberant mouth, fluorescent eyes and no nose or ears. The monster was covered with a scaly, leaflike skin and had two long, spindly arms that almost touched the ground. Years after the incident, Wetzel recalled one other disturbing detail about the creature: its two legs grew out of its sides, instead of at the bottom of its torso.

When the monster spotted Wetzel inside the car, it screeched wildly, leapt onto the hood, and clawed at the windshield with its long arms. Wetzel grabbed his .22 revolver, but then quickly thought better of shooting through the glass barrier, and instead floored his accelerator. As the car began to move, the beast tumbled off, screaming as it was run over.

Wetzel immediately reported this confrontation to the Riverside police. Examining the car, they found that something had left claw-marks on the hood and scraped grease off the car's underside. Policemen and bloodhounds combed the area around the bridge, but found nothing. The following night, however, another terrified motorist showed up at the police station, claiming that a black monster had attacked him at the bridge!

Eighteen years later, 21-inch footprints were found in the Santa Ana River Basin during the mid-Seventies Bigfoot scare. The culprit was assumed to be a Southern California Sasquatch, but it could be that an even stranger creature still lurked around the Santa Ana's bridges and sandbars. Thankfully, it gave up attacking humans back in 1958.

SAN DIEGO COUNTY

Anza-Borrego Desert State Park For sheer volume of strange phenomena, California's largest state park must also be its most mysterious as well:

Agua Caliente Springs (26 mi N of Ocotillo on Hwy S2) Today, the hot and cold springs in this desert canyon are maintained as a county park. Sufferers of arthritis and rheumatism park their mobile homes here for up to six months at a time, to enjoy the springs' soothing waters.

But back in the Thirties, Agua Caliente Springs were known only to a few locals, such as Myrtle and Louis Botts of nearby Julian. Myrtle, an amateur botanist, was especially fond of the springs, since brilliant wildflowers grew in the canyons above them.

In early 1933, she and her husband, on a wildflower hunt here, were camped at the mouth of a canyon, when a dirty old prospector wandered by and told them an amazing story. Up in the canyon a few days earlier, he had seen an old ship sticking out of a sheer mountain wall. When the desert rat then told the Bottses that he had also found Pegleg Smith's legendary lost mine, they thanked him for the information, saw him off, and had a good laugh.

But they weren't laughing the next day. That morning the Bottses hiked into the canyon, and when they passed beyond a steep grade, they saw the forward half of a large, ancient ship poking out of a mountainside, just as the prospector had told them. The vessel had a curved prow, circular marks along its sides where shields had once been, and four deep furrows in the bow. The craft was high above the Bottses, and the mountain wall that held it was a sheer, nearly impassible sheet of shale and clay. The couple noted its exact location, memorized the nearby landmarks in the canyon and excitedly headed back to camp.

Seconds after they returned to their camp, the devastating 1933 earthquake hit with full force. Their campsite was destroyed, so the two returned to their home in Julian.

Myrtle Botts was tantalized by the mysterious wreck, and immediately began to read up on ancient ships at the library where she worked. After several days of study, she decided that the craft most closely resembled one of the old Viking sea raiders, though she couldn't bring herself to believe that Norsemen sailed the ship over 40 miles of mountains to Agua Caliente. She and her husband resolved to visit Agua Caliente Springs the following weekend, and take pictures of the craft to prove it existed.

But when they returned to the canyon, they were stopped short by a slide that blocked the trail where they had hiked a week earlier. There was no trace of the ship or the canyon wall that held it. The Bottses decided that the earthquake had shaken tons of earth loose from the mountain, burying the craft beneath it.

The idea of a Viking ship stranded in the Borrego Desert may not be quite as preposterous as it sounds. During the great Norse expeditionary period from 900-1100 AD, high temperatures in the Northern Hemisphere melted away much of the Arctic ice north of Canada. At least one Viking ship may have sailed through the Northwest Passage there and down through the Bering Strait, though the prevailing east winds in the Arctic guaranteed that the adventurers would never make it back to Scandinavia.

A curious Indian legend implies that Vikings may have strayed as far south as Mexico. The Seri Indians of the Gulf of California's Tiburon Island still tell of the "Come-From-Afar-Men" who landed on the island in a "long boat with a head like a snake." They say the strange men had yellow hair and beards, and a woman with red hair was among them. Their chief stayed on the island with the redheaded woman while his men hunted whales in the Gulf. When they had finished hunting, the strangers went back on their ship and sailed away.

One version of the legend says their ship sank in the Gulf, and the survivors swam ashore and were taken in by the Mayo Indians. Even today, the Mayos sometimes produce children with blond hair and blue eyes, and say that they are descendants of the strangers that married into the tribe in ancient times.

Others say that the fair-haired foreigners sailed farther up the Gulf and were never seen again. If, as some revisionist geographers insist, the Imperial Valley was once an extension of the Gulf of California, then the ship could have run aground on what are now the Tierra Blanca Mountains. So it may lie today buried under tons of earthquake-loosened rock and soil in the canyon above Agua Caliente Springs. (For another account of a legendary desert ship, see **IMPERIAL COUNTY: Salton Sea.**)

Borrego Badlands (8 mi. E of Borrego Springs) For over a century, prospectors have roamed this rough, desolate outback in search of Pegleg Smith's fabulous treasure. One of America's most famous lost gold mines, the legendary Lost Pegleg has lured countless miners, desert rats and dreamers into the Badlands, each one confident that he could locate Smith's fabled lode of black-stained nuggets. To this day nobody's succeeded, though there is a crude memorial four miles northeast of Borrego Springs, at the end of Pegleg Road honoring these adventurers.

Around the turn of the century, when the legend of the Lost Pegleg was most potent, another curious story began to circulate around the Borrego Desert. It seemed that a terrifying phantom was chasing miners out of the Badlands, one of the lost-mine hunters' target areas.

The first man to see the phantom was Charley Arizona, a wise old desert hand who thought he'd seen everything the land could throw at him. One night, Charley was camped on the western edge of the Badlands, when something scared his burros. Walking over to investigate, the prospector spotted an eight-foot tall skeleton stumbling around just 200 yards to the east. The skeleton had a lanternlike light flickering through its ribs, and

Charley swore that he "could hear his bones a-rattlin'" as it disappeared over a ridge.

The phantom showed up again about two years later, when two prospectors saw it in the Superstition Hills to the south. They forgot about the incident until a year afterwards, when another prospector told them he'd seen a giant skeleton with a light in its chest loping aimlessly around the Badlands.

Soon, almost all of Borrego's regulars knew about the strange phantom. Stories and speculations about it made the rounds of the prospectors' fraternity for several years. Eventually two men, whose names are now lost, set out to track down the skeleton for themselves.

They weren't disappointed. On the third night of their hunt, they spotted an eerie light bobbing around in the Borrego Badlands. They approached it, and sure enough, it was the skeleton, running around crazily in the black night. The pair took off after it, chasing the wraith at top speed over hills and through arroyos. One of the men even took a shot at the shambling phantom. But after about three miles, the skeleton lost his pursuers in the dark desert.

The skeleton was seen infrequently afterwards, usually in the Badlands, and a story began to grow up around it. It was, they said, the spirit of a man who had found and worked the appropriately named Phantom Mine, and had died on the desert, his body reduced to bones by scavengers and heat. And his ghost, in the form of a huge skeleton, wanders the night desert around his old claim, chasing off all intruders.

Though the glowing phantom hasn't been seen in recent years, it would still take a brave soul to spend the night in this lonely region, the home of a fabulous treasure and, if the stories are true, a singular desert phantom.

Borrego Sink (4.5 mi SE of Borrego Springs) It's hardly surprising that Bigfoot has been seen on this desert. If the land can house beached Viking ships and eight-foot-tall glow-in-the-dark skeletons, it can certainly provide a home for everybody's favorite North American mystery creature.

Southern California Bigfoot expert Ken Coon once interviewed a man who said he'd seen Sasquatches in the tangle of dry gulches known as Borrego Sink. The man, a store owner who wished to remain anonymous, told Coon that he was prospecting around the Sink back in 1939, camped alone at night, when he was confronted by a pack of hairy, two-legged creatures. The beasts were covered with white or silver fur, and had red eyes that glowed in the dark. They surrounded his camp and menaced him

This desert is home to a legendary lost mine, a glowing giant skeleton and a tribe of Bigfeet.

for some time, but were frightened by his blazing campfire and kept their distance.

Almost 30 years later, Harold Lancaster was also camped near the Sink when he spotted a "giant apeman" walking towards his camp one morning. Lancaster feared that the beast would attack him, so he grabbed his revolver and fired some warning shots into the air. The apeman "jumped a good three feet off the ground" when he heard the reports, then glared in Lancaster's direction, turned tail and ran. The low-desert Sasquatch hasn't been seen since.

Carrizo Wash (16 mi. N of Ocotillo, N of Sweeney Pass on Hwy S2) A Flying Dutchman of the desert haunts the old Butterfield Stage road here, a phantom stagecoach doomed to travel the desert highway for eternity.

Philip Bailey, who collected Borrego's strange tales and legends in his book *Golden Mirages*, recounted how he first heard of the ghostly stage. Bailey was hanging out at the old site of Carrizo, talking to an ancient desert rat, when the man told him that only the other night, an 1860s-era four-mule stage had rumbled along the dark road, carrying only a lone driver and no passengers. The old prospector said he'd first seen the stage on the long-unused trail back in the 1890s.

Bailey then recalled that he'd heard a peculiar story about a stage that disappeared near Carrizo back in the 1860s. The stage was carrying a driver, a guard, and a box of gold bound for San Diego when the guard became ill and got off the stage. The driver then headed out into the desert alone, only to be held up by bandits in the Carrizo Wash, and shot dead. As the driver's body lay slumped over the reins, the team pulled the stage through Carrizo, out to the desert, and into oblivion.

And ever since then, the stage has returned to haunt the Carrizo Wash. They say it leaves wheel ruts in the soft soil as the ghostly driver urges his team on, running full speed towards a destination it will never reach.

Oriflamme Mountain (4 mi W of the Butterfield Ranch on Hwy S2) On dark desert nights, mysterious "ghost lights" often play over the slopes of Oriflamme ("golden flame") Mountain.

These strange lights have been seen in other parts of the Borrego Desert as well. Back in the 1880s, miners said that "burning balls" often lit up the night sky like fireworks over the Vallecito Mountains, in the center of the park. A "spirit light" that bobbed along nearby San Felipe Creek in the 1930s was written up in the American Society for Psychical Research's journal.

For a long time, it was thought that Oriflamme's lights were signal-flares from bootleggers. But the mountain is an exposed, barren ridge of little use to moonshiners, and its glowing balls have long outlived Prohibition.

Others have said that the lights are caused by natural processes. They maintain that dry desert winds blow sand against quartz outcroppings on the mountain, and this produces static electricity that lights the dark slopes with bright flashes. It's a good theory, but it hasn't been proven yet.

Die-hard romantics take a third position. They claim that the glowing orbs on Oriflamme are "money lights." These are the legendary luminous balls, most famous in South America, that mark gold veins and buried treasure. The Borrego desert is probably hiding a few major ore deposits, but nobody's ever followed the lights to them.

Until somebody does, or until an alternative explanation is proven, the strange "ghost lights" will remain a mystery.

Vallecito Station (4 mi W of Agua Caliente Springs on Hwy S2) In the boom years after the California Gold Rush, the Butterfield Stage Line linked San Francisco with St. Louis. Between 1858 and 1861, the line ran passengers and mail between the cities in less than 24 days, a minor miracle of transportation then.

But it was a hard trip. Every rut and pothole in the primitive dirt road hit passengers in the hollows of their joints and the pits of their stomachs. The heat, dust, sweat and boredom soon grew oppressive. There was always the threat of holdups or Indian attacks. And rest stops were infrequent.

Because so many miseries and tensions accumulated on the road, stage stations became the scenes of countless lurid, tragic and violent events. There's hardly one of these landmarks along the old Butterfield Trail that isn't said to contain ghosts, buried treasure, impromptu burial sites or some combination of these.

Vallecito Station, at Vallecito County Park, is no exception. It's haunted by several specters from the old Butterfield days. A phantom white horse sometimes gallops along the road, and the ghosts of two Texans who killed each other in a pointless duel occasionally replay their confrontation on moonlit nights. The Phantom Stage of Carrizo Wash (see entry above) has even been known to rattle by the little adobe every now and then.

But the station's most famous ghost is the "White Lady of Vallecito," a young woman in a white bridal gown who haunts the station at night. In life, she was an Easterner who was traveling to Sacramento to meet her

A phantom horse, dueling ghosts and a "Woman in White" haunt Vallecito Station.

fiance, who had just struck it rich in the gold fields. Along the way, she fell deathly ill, and died at Vallecito Station. When her baggage was opened, her bridal gown was found, and she was dressed in it and buried just down the road.

And in the dark desert nights, she silently paces the adobe grounds, yet another one of California's eerie "Women in White."

Deadman's Hole *(7 mi NW of Warner Springs on Hwy 79)* Back in the 19th century, this wooded hollow witnessed a string of unsolved murders that were blamed on a rampaging Sasquatch.

It all began in 1858, when an unidentified man was slain here. Twelve years later, a Frenchman who had just settled in the Hole was murdered in his cabin. Two more locals were killed at the Hole: prospector David Blair, who was found dead of "knife wounds" in June 1887; and a young woman named Belinda, who was either shot, strangled or mutilated three months later.

The rest of the story is vague and controversial. In March 1888, two hunters from Julian went up into Dark Canyon, just west of the Hole, and were allegedly attacked by "an immense unwieldy animal" that was over six feet tall, covered with black hair, with huge feet and a humanlike face and head. The hunters had been exploring a little cave full of human and animal remains when the creature surprised them. Cornered, they shot it dead.

The beast's body was then supposedly taken to either Julian or San Diego, and exhibited publicly at a police station on April 1. The *San Diego Union* covered the story, and blamed the beast for the recent murders at Deadman's Hole. The next day, though, the paper ran a retraction, dismissing the whole thing as an April Fool's Day joke and belittling credulous readers who had trudged down to the PD to see the monster. If the whole incident was a joke, it was in extremely poor taste, considering that it made light of real, recent murders.

Ugly rumors and feelings still surround Deadman's Hole. Local sportsmen tell of "bad vibes" around the hollow, and Indians give the area a wide berth. Nobody quite knows why the wooded glade still inspires such feelings of dread.

San Diego Two famous haunted houses and a notable geological anomaly can be found in this city, the "birthplace" of California:

Point Loma (SW end of San Diego Bay) Hundreds of "traveled boulders" lie at the low-tide line and along the bluffs here near Cabrillo National Monument.

The huge rocks are not native to the Point Loma soil. The nearest source for similar rock is across 18 miles of ocean, on North Coronado Island. How the rocks, some of which weigh 50 tons and lie 350 feet above sea level, got to the point is a mystery.

Orthodox geologists usually explain away such "erratics" as glacier-borne rock. But glaciers never touched this area.

A more likely theory has it that they were carried here by massive oceanic flooding. This idea is highly unpopular among mainline geologists, since they tend to associate huge, worldwide flooding with the Biblical deluge, and don't want to admit that their fundamentalist-Christian enemies might be right about at least *one* prehistorical event.

Villa Montezuma (1925 K St.) This ornate Victorian mansion, known to its neighbors as "The Spook House," is home to both a brooding ghost and a legendary curse.

The house was built in 1887 by opera singer Jesse Shepard, whose unique talents had made him rich and famous. It was said that Shepard had a vocal range from base to soprano, could sing any part of any opera from memory, and could even sing in two voices at once.

Shepard's incredible talents didn't go unnoticed by high society, and he performed all over Europe for the titled nobility. One of his best engagements was in St. Petersburg, where the Czar's personal medium, General Jourafsky, introduced him to spiritualism, and taught him to conduct seances. An eager student, Shepard later studied occultism under the great Theosophist, Helena Blatvatsky.

When Shepard arrived in San Diego, two wealthy cattllemen named William and John High befriended him, and offered to build him a grand mansion. Their motivation was only partially from friendship and admiration; while the house went up, the High brothers bought up all the property surrounding it, and resold the land at a tidy profit after Shepard's fame spread throughout Southern California.

When the turreted Victorian was completed, Shepard named it the Villa Montezuma, and turned it into the strangest society playground in San Diego. In the music room, where a huge stained-glass window protrayed him as a medieval Crusader, Jesse Shepard performed "musical seances" for the cream of society. They sat in the darkened corners, spellbound as Shepard summoned strange sounds and tones seemingly out of nowhere. The highlight of his act was the "Grand Egyptian March",

San Diego's eerie Villa Montezuma is known for spectral music, a curse and a grieving ghost.

where Shepard, using only his voice and his piano, simulated a full-orchestral battle between two armies. The distinct sounds of a trumpet call, clashing sabers and roaring cannons echoed out of the walls, floor and ceiling, astounding his aristocratic audiences.

Eventually, Shepard tired of performing musical spook shows for San Diego's upper class and moved back to Europe. Years later, he ended up in Los Angeles, and died there, penniless and alone in a run-down hotel room.

After Shepard's departure, a hex fell upon the subsequent owners. Banker D.D. Dare, who bought the house from the opera singer, was accused of embezzling funds from the California National Bank, and dissappeared after his partner committed suicide. The next owner lost the house in a foreclosure after several bad investments. So did the fourth owner, Dr. George M. Calmus, who, like Dare, fled rather than face bankruptcy and eviction.

The last victim of the house's strange jinx was former silent film actress Amelia Jaeger. Living under the house's brooding turrets, Ms. Jaeger went slowly insane, constantly terrified of attack and packing a pistol at all times. She eventually sold the house for half its value, desperate to free herself from its clutches. But a court later voided the transaction, saying that Ms. Jaeger was of unsound mind when she sold the Victorian mansion. Again, she was stuck with the accursed Villa Montezuma.

Today, the house is owned by the City, and open to the public as a museum, though it retains its mysteries. Sensitives have felt Jesse Shepard's "presence" in the music room. And ghostly faces and figures sometimes stare out of the house's many mirrors at startled visitors.

Villa Montezuma's most notorious phantom is the pathetic figure who looks out of the tower windows. He's the ghost of a servant who, devastated by his wife's death, hanged himself in the cupola-topped tower. The ghost has also been seen in the upstairs rooms, and some have even heard his sobbing, piteous moans.

One hundred years after Jesse Shepard entertained San Diegan society at Villa Montezuma, the ghostly sounds continue. Except now, they are not the strange, spectral music that only he could produce, but the lamentations of one of the house's many victims.

Villa Montezuma is open Tues.-Fri. and Sun. from 1-4:30; Phone (619)239-2211.

Whaley House (2482 San Diego Ave., in Old Town State Historic Park) This 130-year old, ghost-ridden building is recognized as an "Official Haunted House" by the State of California.

This honor, shared only by the Winchester Mystery House in San Jose (q.v.), has helped make the Whaley House one of the most famous haunted places in the United States. Opened to the public in 1956, both staff and visitors have seen, heard and smelled all sorts of ghostly emanations from the house's violent past.

The property entered San Diego history as the site of a public execution. A runaway sailor named Yankee Jim Robinson was caught stealing a boat, was wounded during his arrest, and condemned to hang by a drunken judge. Delirious from an infection-induced fever, Yankee Jim couldn't believe the sentence, even when they hauled him up on an improvised gallows on the site where the house now stands. When the wagon Jim stood on was pulled away, the rope failed to snap his neck, and he dangled for almost an hour, cursing and flailing as he slowly strangled.

Later, the property was purchased by transplanted New Yorker Thomas Whaley, and he built the house there in 1857 for himself and his new wife, Anna. Whaley rented part of the house to the county as a courtroom and records storage area, and for several years a variety of local miscreants and criminals were brought to the house to receive frontier justice.

But as San Diego began to grow, tensions flared between Old Towners around the Whaley House and New Towners to the south. New Town residents demanded that the courtroom and records be relocated to their end of the city, but Whaley and other Old Town citizens resisted. When an order was issued to seize County records and courtroom furniture from the Whaley House, the Old Towners responded by declaring martial law, sandbagging Whaley House and surrounding it with armed men. They even mounted a cannon out front.

The confrontation soon turned into a stalemate. Whaley took advantage of the lull in hostilities and made a short business trip to San Francisco.

When word of his absence got out, Old Town's enemies moved into action. They greased their wagons, muffled their horse's hoofs and sneaked over to Whaley House under cover of darkness. The men then stormed into the house, held Whaley's wife and child at gunpoint and stripped the premises of county furniture and records.

Whaley returned a few days later to a ransacked house and a terrified family, and flew into a rage. He wrote a long series of angry letters to the County, castigating them for invading his home and demanding rent and reparations for the damages that the raiders had done. The letters and demands didn't cease until Whaley died 19 years later; none were ever settled.

Anna Whaley lived on in the house until her death in 1913. Lillian, her only child, stayed there 40 years after that, giving up the ghost and the property in 1953.

When the County finally closed the book on the century-old Whaley dispute by purchasing the house and restoring it, odd things began to happen. Workmen told of ghostly footsteps walking on the second floor and the stairs. Soon after the house was finished, windows began to open by themselves, and something kept setting off the burglar alarm in the middle of the night.

English medium Sybil Leek toured the house in 1965. Completely ignorant of the site's history and ghostly disturbances, she communicated with an angry male spirit who said that he had been cheated and wanted justice done. He claimed that he opened the house's windows and

The "haunted spot" where Yankee Jim was hanged.

triggered the burglar alarm so that the world would know he was still master of the house. This could only have been the spirit of Thomas Whaley, still demanding redress from beyond the grave.

Other mediums visited the house, and told of seeing a man hanging at the archway between the front parlor and the music room. Old records showed that it was the exact spot where Yankee Jim met his gruesome end. Some saw prostitutes, sailors and bandits standing before the courtroom bench. One even witnessed the reenactment of a brutal murder in one of the upstairs bedrooms.

Ordinary visitors, too, have experienced strange things. A glass case in the courtroom displays a collection of casual photos taken in the house that reveal balls of light, shadows and even human figures that were invisible to the photographers but somehow showed up on film.

There's also the odor of cigar smoke that's sometimes detected on the ground floor. Smoking is strictly prohibited in the old house, but volunteer workers have never caught a live smoker producing the fumes. All they know is that Thomas Whaley was well known for his love of Havana stogies.

But the most dramatic phenomena at Whaley House are the ghosts' appearances. A mustachioed man in a frock coat sometimes materializes on the stairway, and a small woman in a nightgown occasionally walks the upstairs hallway. They are believed to be the Whaley couple. Other ghosts seen over the years include a spotted dog, a baby (probably Thomas Jr., who died in the house at 17 months), and a little girl whose tiny voice is sometimes heard asking women visitors, "Are you my mama?" She's thought to be the spirit of a child who was accidentally killed in the back yard.

The State Park volunteers are unfazed by all the strange phenomena in the house. They brush off encounters with the resident phantoms as just another fact of life in the Whaley House. Most have seen the strange forms, heard the ghostly voices and smelled the untraceable odors, and they aren't afraid to tell visitors, or tell off ghosts.

One volunteer told the author that she had been dusting furniture in the Music Room when a disembodied male voice demanded of her, "What...are...you...doing?" Without batting an eyelash, missing a beat, or looking up from her work, she answered calmly, "I'm dusting." The voice spoke no more.

It's all in a day's work at the haunted Whaley House.

The Whaley House is open Wed.-Sun. from 10-4:30. Phone: (619) 298-2482.

Bibliography

Allen, Stuart S. "Forest of Disappearing Children." *Fate* 14 (Jul. 1961): 36-41.

Aveni, Anthony F., ed. *Archaeoastronomy in Pre-Columbian America.* Austin, Tex.: Univ. of Texas, 1975.

Bailey, Philip. *Golden Mirages.* New York: Macmillan, 1940.

Bell, Horace. *On the Old West Coast.* New York: William Morrow & Co., 1930.

Bentor, Y.K., and Kastner, M. "Combustion Metamorphism in Southern California." *Science* 193 (6 Aug. 1976): 486-88.

Berkeley Gazette, March 19, 1974.

Bord, Janet. *Mazes and Labyrinths of the World.* New York: Dutton, 1975.

Bord, Janet and Colin. *The Bigfoot Casebook.* Harrisburg, Pa.: Stackpole, 1982.

Brandon, Jim. *Weird America.* New York: Dutton, 1978.

——*The Rebirth of Pan.* Dunlap, Ill.: Firebird, 1983.

Brisbane, Howard H. "U.S. Navy Meets a Phantom Ship." *Fate* 15 (Apr. 1962): 41-44.

Calico Early Man Archaeological Site. Washington, DC: U.S. Government Printing Office, 1984.

"Case-Record of a Vanished Civilization in the Californian Area." *Journal of the American Society for Psychical Research* 28 (1934): 292.

Cerve, Wishar S. [Harve Spencer Lewis]. *Lemuria, the Lost Continent of the Pacific.* San Jose, Calif.: Rosicrucian Press, 1931.

Coleman, Loren. *Mysterious America.* Winchester, Mass.: Faber & Faber, 1983.

——*Curious Encounters.* Winchester, Mass.: Faber & Faber, 1985.

Corliss, William. *Ancient Man: A Handbook of Puzzling Artifacts.* Glen Arm, Md.: Sourcebook Project, 1978.

Curran, Douglas. *In Advance of the Landing: Folk Concepts of Outer Space.* New York: Abbeville, 1985.

Derr, John S. "Earthquake Lights: A Review of Observations and Present Theories." *Bulletin of the Seismic Society of America* 63 (1973): 2177-87.

—— "Earthquake Lights." *Earthquake Information Bulletin* 9 (May-Jun. 1977): 18-21.

Eberhart, George. *A Geo-Bibliography of Anomalies.* Westport, Conn.: Greenwood, 1980.

Eichorn, Arthur F. *The Mount Shasta Story.* Mount Shasta, Calif.: The Herald, 1957.

Ellwood, Robert S., Jr. *Religious and Spiritual Groups in Modern America.* Englewood Cliffs, N.J.: Prentice Hall.

Eureka (Calif.) Humboldt Times, Jan. 24 & Sep. 1, 1960.

Folsom, Franklin. *America's Ancient Treasures.* New York: Rand McNally, 1974.

Fort, Charles. *The Complete Books of Charles Fort.* Mineola, N.Y.: Dover, 1974.

Fry, Al. "1987 High Desert Encounters." *INFO Journal,* no. 53 (Sep. 1987), p.29.

Fuller, Curtis. "The Endless Search." *Fate* 23 (Nov. 1970): 32-36.

Gaddis, Vincent. *Mysterious Fires and Lights.* New York: Dell, 1968.

"The Ghost of Clear Lake." *Fate* 8 (Jul. 1955): 22.

Green, John. *On the Track of the Sasquatch.* New York: Ballantine, 1973.

—— *The Sasquatch File.* Agassiz, B.C.: Cheam, 1973.

—— *Sasquatch: The Apes Among Us.* Cheam: 1978.

Hallan-Gibson, Pamela. *The Golden Promise: An Illustrated History of Orange County.* Northridge, Calif.: Windsor, 1986.

Heuvelmans, Bernard. *In the Wake of the Sea-Serpents.* New York: Hill & Wang, 1968.

Holzer, Hans. *Ghosts of the Golden West.* New York: Ace, 1968.

Keel, John. *Strange Creatures from Time and Space.* Greenwich, Conn.: Fawcett, 1970.

Leadabrand, Russ. "Let's Explore a Byway: Along the Butterfield Trail." *Westways* 53 (Apr. 1961): 4-6.

Lee, Hector. *Heroes, Villains and Ghosts: Folklore of Old California.* Santa Barbara, Calif.: Capra, 1984.

Los Angeles Herald-Examiner, May 12, 13, 14 and 15, 1982.

Los Angeles Times, Jan. 29, 1934; Jun. 17, 1982.

Lovelace. Leland. *Lost Mines and Hidden Treasure.* San Antonio, Tex.: Naylor, 1956.

MacLellan, Alec. *The Lost World of Agharti.* London: Souvenir, 1982.

Marinacci, Barbara and Rudy. *Take Sunset Boulevard.* San Rafael, Calif.: Presidio, 1980.

Marshall, Gen. George C. "Giant Effigies of the Southwest." *National Geographic* 102 (Sep.1952): 389.

May, Antoinette. *Haunted Houses and Wandering Ghosts of California.* San

Francisco: Examiner Special Projects, 1977.

Mertz, Henriette. *Pale Ink*. Chicago: Swallow, 1973.

Mortensen, C.E., and Johnston, M.J.S. "Anomalous Tilt Proceeding the Hollister Earthquake of November 28, 1974." *Journal of Geophysical Research* 81 (1976): 3561-66.

Myers, Arthur. *The Ghostly Register*. Chicago: Contemporary, 1986.

O'Brien, Robert. *This is San Francisco*. New York: Whittlesey House, 1948.

Orange County Register, Sep. 27, 1987.

Phylos the Tibetan [Frederick S. Oliver]. *A Dweller on Two Planets*. Los Angeles: Borden, 1940.

Reinstedt, Randall. *Ghosts, Bandits and Legends of Old Monterey*. Carmel, Calif.: Ghost Town, 1974.

—— *Ghostly Tales and Mysterious Happenings of Old Monterey*. Ghost Town, 1977.

—— *Mysterious Sea Monsters of California's Central Coast*. Ghost Town, 1977.

Sacramento Union, May 17, 1971.

San Francisco Chronicle, Oct. 17, 30, 1976; Feb. 18, Sep. 9, 1979; Oct. 31, 1980; Oct. 12, 17, 1981; Mar. 7, 1983; Jul. 12, Oct. 28, Dec. 31, 1984; Aug. 13, Oct. 31, 1985.

Scheffer, Victor B. "The Mystery of the Mima Mounds." *Scientific Monthly* 65 (Oct. 1947): 283-294.

Senate, Richard. *Ghosts of the Haunted Coast*. Ventura, Calif.: Pathfinder, 1985.

Setzler, Frank M. "Seeking the Secret of the Giants." *National Geographic* 102 (Sep. 1952): 390-404.

Smith, Susy. *Prominent American Ghosts*. New York: Dell, 1969.

Strickler, Carolyn. "Haunting Shadows of Leonis." *Westways* 71 (Oct. 1979): 46-48.

Webb, Richard. *Great Ghosts of the West*. Los Angeles: Nash, 1971.

Weight, Harold O. "A Desert Ship that Wasn't Lost." *Westways* 56 (May 1964): 32-33.

—— "He Saw the Lost Desert Ship." *Westways* 57 (Nov. 1965): 11-13.

—— "Charley Clusker and the Lost Ship." *Desert* 40 (Mar. 1977): 32-37.

White, Betty Lou. "The Ghosts of Fresno." *Fate* 20 (Aug. 1967): 83-85.

Williams, Brad, and Pepper, Choral. *The Mysterious West*. New York: World, 1967.

—— *Lost Legends of the West*. New York: Holt, Rinehart & Winston, 1970.

Winer, Richard, and Osborn, Nancy. *Haunted Houses*. New York: Bantam, 1979.

Index

ORDER FORM

Panpipes Press
P.O. Box 25226
Los Angeles, CA 90025-0226 USA
Phone (213) 207-0832

Please send me ____ copies of **Mysterious California**. I am enclosing $7.95 per copy. **Postage and handling** is $1.50 for the first book and 50¢ for each additional book. **Californians:** Please add 52¢ per book to cover sales tax.

I understand that I may return the book for a full refund if not satisfied.

Name:_____

Address:_____

City:_____ State:_____ Zip:_____

____ Please rush my book(s) via First Class Mail. I am enclosing **$3.00** per book for this service.